Filling Our Father's House

Shaun McAfee

Filling Our Father's House

What Converts Can Teach Us about Evangelization

SOPHIA INSTITUTE PRESS
Manchester, New Hampshire

Sophia Institute Press
Box 5284, Manchester, NH 03108
1-800-888-9344

www.SophiaInstitute.com

Sophia Institute Press® is a registered trademark of Sophia Institute.

Library of Congress Cataloging-in-Publication Data

McAfee, Shaun A.

Filling our father's house : what converts can teach us about evangelization / Shaun A. McAfee.

pages cm

Includes bibliographical references and index.

ISBN 978-1-62282-236-2 (alk. paper)

1. Catholic Church—Apologetic works. 2. Catholic converts. 3. Protestant churches—Doctrines. 4. Catholic Church—Doctrines. 5. Protestant churches—Relations—Catholic Church. 6. Catholic Church—Relations—Protestant churches. I. Title.

BX1752.M45 2014

282—dc23

2014034927

First printing

To my wife, Jessica

Contents

Anything wrought by the grace of the Holy Spirit in the hearts of our separated brethren can be a help to our own edification. Whatever is truly Christian is never contrary to what genuinely belongs to the faith; indeed, it can always bring a deeper realization of the mystery of Christ and the Church.

—*Unitatis Redintegratio*, no. 4

Foreword

It's not always easy to recognize and appreciate good things when we encounter them. This is especially true when you stumble across something of value that you never expected to be there on the path. It's tempting to keep moving and not bother to pause and inspect that bump in the road.

Russell H. Conwell's famous story "Acres of Diamonds" is an allegory of how easily we overlook—to our own detriment—good things that are all around us simply because we don't take time to notice them. Conwell describes a nineteenth-century farmer who sold his farm and equipment to finance his dream of getting rich as a diamond miner. He ventured far off to the diamond mines and, even after many years of hardscrabble effort, never found any diamonds, much less made a fortune on them. Eventually, penniless, exhausted, and filled with despair and disillusionment, he committed suicide by drowning himself in a river.

The man who bought that unsuccessful miner's farm, however, had a very different life. One day, as he trudged through his fields, this farmer noticed an odd and interesting rock about the size of an orange protruding from the dirt. After cleaning the dirt off, he displayed the rock as a curiosity in his living room.

A visitor happened to take a close look at the rock and, to his shock and awe, realized it was in fact a humongous diamond. Breathlessly, he asked the farmer if he had seen other "rocks" like this one.

"Yes, of course," the farmer chuckled. "There are hundreds of them strewn all over the place. Why?"

It turns out that the unusual rock was the biggest diamond ever found in those parts, and, to the farmer's joyful amazement, there were countless more of them just waiting to be picked up off the ground.

The moral of this story? If you don't look for and discern the hidden value in the everyday things and people in your life, you will ineluctably miss out on opportunities to acquire new skills, deepen your knowledge, benefit from others' experiences, and receive blessings from God, all of which are apt to make you a better person, a wiser and more virtuous Christian, and a more efficacious apostle for Jesus Christ.

Sometimes, like that proverbial diamond in the rough, something precious and important may be obscured by the debris and dross that surrounds it — perhaps the taxing personality of someone who rubs you the wrong way, or the irritating fact that someone you think couldn't *possibly* know something you do not know does know it, or the humbling realization that the path toward becoming a better and holier Christian lies chiefly in the ordinary things of this life.

And *those* are the things we so often and so easily overlook, are they not?

This book can help you greatly in that regard as it shines a needed spotlight on weighty but, for some Catholics, often forgotten essentials of the Christian life, such as the following:

Foreword

- *evangelically* sharing (yes, sharing!) the Faith with others, so many of whom hunger and thirst for the truth, perhaps, without even consciously realizing it

- the practical implications of Jesus' command to "love one another," including and especially those who might look down on you and reject you for being Catholic

- the commission to share with those around you the awesome, holy, saving power of God's grace working in your own life, especially in the Holy Eucharist, confession, and the other sacraments

- the importance of reading and assimilating the life-giving, life-changing truths imparted by the Holy Spirit in the Holy Bible, and much more

Perhaps that is how this excellent book can benefit you the most: by drawing to your attention to these aspects of an authentically *Catholic* life that the saints have always known and made use of in their efforts to shine forth and speak forth the truth of Jesus Christ but, in recent generations, have become lost to us, things that many Catholics have, sadly, forgotten about.

Let's relearn those skills. Let's love and ponder and master the ways and means of communicating the timeless truths of the Catholic Faith in a modern idiom to a modern audience who has barely, if at all, heard them before.

The more we Catholics recognize and adopt those legitimately and historically Catholic talents and techniques for evangelization, the more we *re-appropriate* and assimilate them into our own lives, the more "diamonds" lying all around us we can scoop up and add to that treasure in heaven that neither moth nor rust consumes nor thieves can break in and steal (cf. Matt. 6:19).

— Patrick Madrid, host of the
Right Here, Right Now radio show,
author of *Why Be Catholic?*

Preface

I am a convert to the Catholic Church.

What does that mean? In my case, it means that I found extraordinary truth, much to my surprise and frankly at one time to my dismay, in the teachings and hospitality of the Catholic Church. That does not mean I did not find good teachings and hospitality while a Protestant. It simply means that I came to be very convinced that the Catholic Church is the Church that Jesus founded, that she has held the same teachings since her foundation, and that the claims of authority are not her own but those of Christ.

While a Protestant I found myself engaged, active, and happy. None of that has changed since I became a Catholic.

I decided to write this book while on the doorstep of a fellow parishioner one Cornhusker football morning. If you know anything about Nebraskans, you know about their love of watching Husker football on a Saturday morning, so having this parishioner speak to me at length when he could have been watching the game was worthy of mention.

What was I doing there? My parish, St. Robert Bellarmine in Omaha, Nebraska, is home to a group based on the successful book *Forming Intentional Disciples* by Sherry Weddell.

Filling Our Father's House

The group serves the function of going door-to-door to engage existing parishioners on behalf of the pastor, receiving prayer requests, listening to concerns, and doing anything else of immediate use to each person or family. Highest of our priorities, though, is to offer each person or family a renewed relationship with Jesus.

Catholics going door-to-door to evangelize? Believe it!

Taking the New Evangelization to the doors of our parishioners, my good friend and I listened to one of our faithful discuss the time he had spent recently in an Episcopal church. He had attended services at that church a couple of Sundays to support his extended family who were parishioners there. He made a point about how inviting that church was and that he felt a sense of being welcome that is not always felt at our parish or in many Catholic parishes.

He reiterated that he didn't feel that Catholics were doing anything wrong, but there was more that our parish and its members could do to show that they weren't just showing up for Mass because they were obligated to. Specifically he told me it was a nice change of pace to have *parishioners* hold the church doors open, shake his hand when he entered the church, and extend good wishes to him as he was leaving.

Talking to my fellow parishioner at his front door got me thinking: someone ought to say something. There are many things Catholics could do that would empower them with a more vibrant outlook on evangelism, aid them in sharing their Faith with others, and create a more hospitable parish community that is, as Pope Francis has recently stated, more "attractive."[1] And so, in the following pages, drawing from Scripture, from

---

[1] *Evangelii Gaudium*, no. 39.

Preface

Magisterial documents, and from my experience, I offer some practical solutions that will lead to a stronger desire for God and His Word and a more successful and vibrant evangelism. These suggestions will also show parish leaders, both lay and pastoral, how to make the changes necessary to engage in a more effective New Evangelization.

Acknowledgments

There are so many people who assisted in the creation of this book that I cannot list them all by name.

First, God. I wouldn't have written this book if I didn't think that its words would be useful to at least one person. I have God to thank for the endurance it has taken to wade through some sicknesses, an ever mounting list of responsibilities I somehow volunteer to undertake, and a family I am lovingly committed to each day. All of this I do in reflection of my blessings, my hope, and my love for and from the Lord. *Thank You, Jesus, for giving me a new chance every day to do a little better, to do a little more good in the world even when I am not up to task.*

A special thanks to my wife, Jessica, who has supported me like no other. She has given me encouragement when I was downcast, counsel when appropriate, and straightforward criticism when it was needed. She might stand at only five foot two, but Jessica is a bold, honest, unshakable woman who is confident and firm in her foundations, and she has always given me inspiration to be a better man. *Thank you, Jessica, for supporting me course after course, season after season, in my study to be a better servant in the Church.*

I could not be the Christian I am today, a convert to the Catholic Church, without first having the privilege of being mentored by my previous pastors. Jeff Wall and Jeff Howe in Fairbanks, Alaska, had a profound impact on my life and showed me how to be a man by example, not just by words. Although we are of different faiths now, I know we are joined in the Body of Christ.

The incredible education I have received so far has been blessed by the graduate faculty and staff at Holy Apostles College and Seminary in Cromwell, Connecticut. This is what I call the best secret in Catholic higher education. The level of scholarship and spiritual development one receives from this school is priceless. It has simply been an honor and a privilege to attend.

Three people I have become friends with at Holy Apostles have assisted and supported me and deserve warm thanks. Dr. Sebastian Mahfood, O.P., vice president of administration, who works in every possible way to bring the school to further superiority and excellence, has mentored and supported me. Dr. Stacy Trasancos, blogger extraordinaire and author of *Science Was Born of Christianity*, whom I look up to in many ways, gets my sincere thanks for helping me become a writer. Professor Judith Babarsky, who has befriended me and mentored me with such enthusiasm, helped me develop as a student and a writer and also put forth many hours in editing and suggesting content for this book.

My thanks are also extended to Dr. Kevin Vost, author of *Memorize the Faith*, *The One-Minute Aquinas*, and *Memorize the Reasons*, and also Shane Kapler, author of *Through, With, and In Him*. Both have been generous as mentors and supporters.

I want to thank Patrick Madrid for his direct involvement in the book. A man who does not let the grass grow under his feet, Patrick, amid all his busyness and obligations, made

Acknowledgments

time to provide suggestions in writing style and content, as well as taking the time and effort to provide the foreword for this book. He is a true apostle. I offer my sincere gratitude for his kindness.

Filling Our Father's House

1

Understand the Need
for Evangelization

An evangelizer must never look like someone
who has just come back from a funeral!

—Pope Francis, *Evangelii Gaudium*, no. 10

There is a growing enthusiasm in Catholicism. Young men and women are taking to the parish and to the Internet in an effort to evangelize and teach their friends, families, and complete strangers about the Faith. They are proclaiming the gospel. Out of this effort many are coming into the Church with zeal, and others are rediscovering their love for the Church. New converts to the Church are excited about their new home—a healthy and active place where the fields are "ripe for harvest" (cf. John 4:35).

In addition to this growth, there is also a decline as the Catholic Church loses members to other persuasions and to apathy. Catholics are leaving because they feel their faith is dead or no longer relevant, or they are convinced that faith and science are incompatible, or they concoct a different reason for their departure. Those who leave the Catholic Church for another Christian faith, albeit Protestant, are missing the fullness of the Faith. In case they missed it the first time, they are in need of evangelization, or if their faith has become deadened, they need a New Evangelization.

The word *evangelism* has a connotation that instantly connotes "Protestant" for many Catholics. As with the door-to-door ministry I mentioned in the preface, the Catholic might think, "Isn't that something Protestants do?" Yes, it is, but evangelism shouldn't be what *only* Protestants do.

The *Merriam-Webster Dictionary* lists two definitions of *evangelize*; one is "to convert to Christianity." That definition doesn't reveal the fullness of what evangelism is. A convert might adopt a new creed, a new belief, but after that, where does his faith take him? Does he simply show up at Mass and other events as a convert, or does he participate? Is his faith on fire? Has he been evangelized? *Merriam-Webster's* other definition of *evangelize* meets the Christian orientation much better with "to preach the gospel to." What powerful words those are! Preach the good news that Jesus Christ has risen from the grave and conquered death, reconciling the whole world to Himself and offering eternal salvation as, finally, the gates of heaven are open to all men! One who is proclaiming this news is surely evangelizing.

Many Catholics prefer to keep faith under their coats. They might believe, but they don't display their belief. And what's worse, once many Catholics make the Sign of the Cross and utter, "Thanks be to God," and the Mass is over, they leave their faith at the door. It's not evangelism. It's not attractive. It's not a proclamation. I had a boss who told me something along the lines of "You have to leave your religion out of your work," to which I replied, "Then it's not a religion at all!"

This is a problem our Church is suffering from. Whether holding grudges or happier elsewhere, some Catholics have left the Church and don't see a reason to come back. Many who haven't left the Church are still malnourished or just aren't interested in deepening their faith and devotion. They have no interest in the apostolate either. They aren't excited about their Faith. They don't comprehend the incredible gift of the Eucharist and don't think the Church has a relative place in society or in daily life. "It might have had that context at one point, but this is the twenty-first century!" some say. Some cradle Catholics lack appreciation for the Faith; because Catholicism is all they have ever known, they are satisfied with their level of involvement or noninvolvement.

Some people have married into the Catholic Church. They attended the required RCIA classes and had no problem with the rites. The things they learned were understood but might not have had any personal impact on their conscious and spiritual life. Because it was a requirement for getting married, or they needed to join the parish the rest of the family belonged to, they adopted the Faith without a complaint but soon stopped attending Mass.

Still other reasons might cause Catholics to fall away from the Church. During confession, a priest might come off as uncaring, insensitive, or downright callous to a penitent. Some might be scandalized by hypocritical acts or mismanagement of funds and donations. Some simply haven't been inspired to act on their faith. Whatever the reason, good or bad, it was enough for them to leave.

What's the concern for the faithful Catholic? You might be a Catholic who goes to Mass each week, observes holy days, and makes a confession when needed. However, not every Catholic does. Numerous Catholics are merely "going through the motions," unaware of the tremendous gifts they have. That ought to concern good, faithful Catholics. No family is ever happy or ambivalent when a member is in a rough place, is sick, or feels unwanted, just as no one is satisfied with a part of his body having an infection or being broken. It matters even more for those who are Christian because we identify with the reality that we are Christ's Body.

Catholics who have left the Church or are eyeing the door, thinking of leaving, are the ones who are in desperate need of evangelization. There needs to be a "new evangelization" because clearly, many did not receive the *old evangelization*. Either way, they need to get back that spark and have their faith reignited.

The New Evangelization

What we know now as the New Evangelization takes root in the Kerygmatic movement, advanced by a group of accomplished 1950s scholars and aimed at urging the Church's clergy to renew the voice of the gospel found in the New Testament by once again taking up the missionary role of the Church as the central focus of her efforts. Later, in 1990, Pope John Paul II wrote the following in his encyclical *Redemptoris Missio* ("Mission of the Redeemer"):

> I sense that the moment has come to commit all the Church's energies to a new evangelization.... No believer in Christ, no institution of the Church can avoid this supreme duty: to proclaim Christ to all peoples. (no. 3)

I can't discern whether people knew at that time what the words *new evangelization* would come to mean for Catholics. Since I have become a Catholic, it appears to be the single most discussed topic among all ministries within the Church and in personal faith. Is it revival? Is it contradicting the implied "old evangelization"? It shouldn't be classified as either. It is more of a renewal of the enthusiasm for the battle against the secularism that is eating away at the sense of God even in the Church. The idea that we are to see God in all that we do, to work in each moment as though we are working for the Lord (cf. Col. 3:23–24), and to acknowledge Him as the Lord is diminishing. The New Evangelization is therefore a kind of renaissance and revitalization in the Church.

The United States Conference of Catholic Bishops tells us:

> The New Evangelization calls each of us to deepen our faith, believe in the Gospel message and go forth to proclaim the Gospel. The focus of the New Evangelization calls all Catholics to be evangelized and then go forth to evangelize.[2]

In these pages you will find ways to deepen your faith and indeed be evangelized — through considering the Catholic Faith in your life, reading Scripture, growing closer to the Lord, and working with others and with your parish to develop your spiritual life — so that you may more confidently and zealously go forth to evangelize.

---

[2] Http://www.usccb.org/beliefs-and-teachings/how-we-teach/new-evangelization/.

2

Develop and Deliver Your Personal Testimony

Go home to your friends, and tell them how much the Lord has done for you, and how he has had mercy on you.

—Mark 5:19

A testimony? You mean I have to tell people about myself? Yes!

Every child of God has a story worth hearing, and Catholics are no exception. There are many wonderful Catholics in the world who love to share their experiences, their conversions, their reversions, and the great works God has done in their lives.

The opportunity to tell your story will come in many different ways. Someone may notice the crucifix hanging around your neck or the picture of Jesus in your home and see the opportunity to ask you about your faith. Other times, you might be faced with the need to be an apologist, being called to defend your faith when one objects to a political or religious conviction you have. The ways and times that you will be able to share your faith are more numerous than the verses in the Bible. One thing remains, though, as St. Peter tells us: you must "always be prepared to make a defense to any one who calls you to account for the hope that is in you" (1 Pet. 3:15).

When it comes to evangelizing, your testimony is the biggest tool in your chest—and also your most useful and necessary tool. Our Lord's last command to us was to, "Go therefore and make disciples of all nations" (Matt. 28:19). In carrying out this "Great Commission," the first step is to entice people to want to be Christian. You can do that through your testimony.

Your testimony is the first thing that people will learn about your Christian faith and the last thing they will remember. This is why you should take time to develop your testimony. Long after the book is read and put back on the shelf, long after the debate is watched once on YouTube, people remember one thing: the story. The impact of a personal story penetrates audiences and individuals like nothing else.

Your testimony is the story of you, your relationship with Christ, and how your faith has affected your life. This chapter will focus on the building blocks of your testimony: how to develop it, how to perfect it, and how to share it. If you follow these guidelines, your testimony will help you be more powerful and effective in sharing your faith with others.

Before I begin discussing the details of how to develop and deliver your personal testimony, I want to tell you, by way of example, about my life as a Christian and eventual conversion to Catholicism.

My Journey Home

Growing up in a military household gave me a humorous outlook on Catholics. We shared the base chapel with Catholics, so I was able to see them taking down their candles, there was sometimes a smell of incense left over in the air, and I remember hearing that Catholics consumed real wine. One day I noticed the kneelers and thought they were footrests. I pulled one down, and my mom told me, "Those are for the Catholics." I remember thinking, "Catholics are fun. They drink real wine, light candles, they have smoke, their services are shorter, and now they have footrests."

But while growing up, I didn't spend much time thinking about the Catholic Church or any particular church, for that matter. My military family moved every three or four years, so we continually found ourselves in a different congregation. We shopped around for the best we could find. My parents, like many other Protestants, searched for a pastor or a chaplain who preached a message that "fed" them.

A pastor we particularly enjoyed was Chaplain Spence in Hawaii. He challenged my family to read through the Bible — or at least through the New Testament — in one year and laid out a simple plan for doing so. Under the leadership of my dad, we made a commitment to spend time reading the New Testament as a family each night. Each of us four children took turns reading an amount he could handle. As the youngest and a slow reader, I seldom read more than a chapter at a time.

Yes, we secretly wanted to get away from that table and play Sega Genesis, but there was something engaging about what we were doing. Even as a nine- or ten-year-old, I was stimulated by the questions my parents would ask. When we got toward the end of Matthew, my mom asked us, "Are you excited to find out what happened to Jesus?" I remember being the only one who didn't know that Jesus was about to be crucified; I learned that the next day, and it broke my heart. I was young and naive but I was beginning to understand.

That memory is typical of those I have of my earlier experiences in the Church. The location changed, but the message seemed fairly consistent. I was happiest when our family was involved, but that wasn't always possible given our circumstances. Then, for some reason, when I was about fifteen years old, my family suddenly stopped attending church. I was happy to take a break and have Sundays to sleep in; I was an apathetic teen.

A year or so later, my good friend and constant companion, James, invited me to Life Teen, a Wednesday night gathering at his Catholic church, St. Andrew's. We went to hang out, to play around, and to talk in small groups. The social fellowship lasted about an hour, and then everyone went to Mass. I followed along.

I wondered what I was doing there. Why were the kids waving smoke around? Why were they doing calisthenics in their seats — sit, stand, kneel — every five minutes? Why were they forming an orderly line to go receive Holy Communion? Didn't they know people sell stackable plates that hold little cups with wine or juice? They could have passed that plate around, not having to get up at all! It was so unfamiliar and strange to me. In the rear of the church, I saw an altar or shrine. It was apparently dedicated to the Virgin Mary, but I didn't question it further. I didn't question any of this for nearly ten years. But I had fun.

At Life Teen, there was another high school student, Richard Rivera, who must have been a volunteer. One evening he took me aside, and cutting to the chase, he told me that if I ever wanted to know more about the Faith or about developing a personal relationship with Jesus, all I had to do was ask him. He gave me his card. I didn't think about that moment for years until I became a Catholic myself, but now it stands out as one of the sincerest gestures I can remember: he looked me in the eye, his hand on my shoulder, and offered me a simple invitation to ask a question whenever I wanted to do so. I have often wondered what became of Richard Rivera.[3]

Eventually I quit going to Life Teen. Nobody offended me, and I left for no particular reason. I just stopped going.

During this time, I still didn't think much about the differences between me and the Catholics I had met or the people of other denominations I knew of. My family lived within a quarter mile of a church; I could see its top from my front door. It was right there, so close, so convenient, so I asked my dad, "Why don't we go to that church? It looks pretty nice, and it's close."

He replied, "Because they're Anglicans. We aren't Anglican." That was a good enough answer for me. I never questioned it again. I didn't even know what an Anglican was. I had never wondered why we had to be a certain denomination to go to a certain church or even what the differences were. It just didn't matter to me.

I didn't return to church until I was an adult. One May, on the drive home after a bonfire on the Tanana River in Fairbanks, Alaska, I was sitting in the backseat of a Ford Ranger, and in that moment I knew I needed a change and asked Jesus to come into my heart. I told God, "I'm not even sure what to do tomorrow, but I will try to listen."

Right away, I got as involved as I could in my chosen church, Friends Community Church in Fairbanks. I listened intently to the sermons and did everything I could to be included in whatever was happening. It was there that I learned to know God,

---

[3] I tracked down Richard Rivera as I wrote this book in late 2013. He is happily in charge of that Life Teen program and of the youth activities at St. Andrew's in Sierra Vista, Arizona. He is a charming and charismatic young man.

to pray about everything, to cry once in a while, and to treat everyone as if he were Jesus Himself. The pastoral team, Jeff Wall and Jeff Howe, were busy men, but they always made time for me. Holy and friendly, the duo attracted me to the gospel like nothing else at the time.

After I had been discharged from the Air Force (my reason for being in Alaska in the first place), my new wife, Jessica, and I moved to North Dakota, where I would finish earning my bachelor's degree. I threw myself into the course work. Three back-to-back-to-back killer semesters with double the full course loads, I was gunning to finish and get out of Dodge. I graduated in 2010, and after a move to Arizona, we were back in Alaska. After much searching, finally, I got a call offering me a job in Omaha, Nebraska. I felt I had no choice but to say yes; I needed the job, and Jessica and I wanted a baby. It was time to settle down somewhere.

We drove into Omaha in mid-December 2010, checked into a hotel, ordered a pizza, and popped on the TV. On came a program with nuns praying. I immediately turned the channel, thinking, "I will never be part of that godforsaken religion," referring to the Catholic Church; I had become quite proud of what I had learned about the history of Christianity and accomplished in study thus far. I had taken courses on Old Testament Scripture, New Testament Scripture, church history, and the Reformation. I knew the arguments, I knew the players—Knox, Calvin, Zwingli, Melanchthon, Luther, and others. I understood the Peasants' Revolt, the vastly different time of feudalism, and the tectonic shift in politics, culture, and thought leading up to and during the Reformation. I even knew of the Counter-Reformation and its players. I reasoned that if the Reformers couldn't get it right and agree, how should I expect to figure it out? Considering the successive schisms, I made sense of the biblical interpretation issues by concluding, "No man can know it all without trumping Jesus Himself. How could man know everything about truth and morals?" Thus, I reasoned it was okay not to have a firm answer concerning the Eucharist, the authority of the pope, or the need for a pope at all.

It wasn't until months later that my wife bought me the *Apologetics Bible*. With more than a hundred essays on Scripture and notes on interpretation, this Bible was exactly what I wanted. I started a blog called *Up with Your Cross* to make a daily offering to anyone willing to read about the Faith for which many are still persecuted today. My blog wasn't a hit at all, but I was engaged. More importantly, I started challenging myself on the bigger issues that separate Christians.

I was seeing a psychologist to work out some personal issues. Focus on the Family, a powerful Protestant ministry, had referred me to Dr. Sean Stevens, and he and I had hit it off from the start. But something bothered me about the way he referred to biblical figures. He called Paul "St. Paul" and referred to Mary as the "Blessed Virgin." I had a feeling he was Catholic, so the next week I asked him plainly, "Sean, you keep saying 'Saint this' and 'Saint that.' Are you Catholic?" Indeed he was. Then I asked him, rather matter-of-factly, "Should I be Catholic?" I wanted to challenge him. His answer astonished me.

"Well, Shaun, I know you love the Lord. I don't doubt your salvation or anything"—he paused to choose his words with care—"but I would say that as a Protestant you don't have all the tools of the faith."

What "Tools" Did I Need?

From there our meetings took a different turn. We had an hour together, and we would start with my personal needs, but then

I would be triggered by a question regarding the "tools of the faith."

"Sean, what are the 'tools' of Catholicism?"

"Shaun, you see, you and I pray together here, but you have many saints and angels to help you pray."

"Seriously?"

"Yes, just like you ask me to pray for you as an intercessor, they can pray for you as well."

I didn't accept what he was telling me. He was clever, but I was determined to find some holes in his persuasion. To my amazement, he put up with me. I argued quite emphatically for my positions, but Sean was always gentle. He didn't just explain a doctrine but gave incredible examples of historical events. In response to my inquiry about the need for confession, he told me about St. John Vianney, a parish priest who endured many hours of hearing confessions each day and had a reputation for knowing even the unconfessed sins of some penitents. I recall the story of a married man who took his life by jumping off a bridge. The man's distressed wife hurried to Vianney, but before she could reach him, he called out to her from the midst of the crowd, "He is saved. Between the parapet and the water, he made an act of contrition" and allayed her fears.[4]

Sean was convincing, and better yet, the stories he told to illustrate the teaching were inspiring. He would tell me about Irenaeus and other early Christians and what they believed and wrote about. My wife had a church history book, and each night I would read up on the primitive Church. What I found amazed me.

---

[4] You can read about this story in François Trochu's biography of St. John Vianney, *The Cure D'Ars.*

The next time Sean and I met, I said, "You mean to tell me that Christians in the first century—who were known to have walked with the Apostles—believed in infant baptism, regeneration at baptism, and that they believed Communion bread was really the Body and Blood of Jesus?" Even more dismayed, I found out that St. Ignatius of Antioch, in his letter to the Smyrnaeans, used the term *Catholic* in about A.D. 110 and wrote about bishops and other offices. Why did that church look so much like the Catholic Church today?

Each week it was a different "stump the Catholic" question. When my wife picked me up, I had to tell her the latest thing. This was the last thing my wife wanted to hear because, as she rightly pointed out, I wasn't paying a psychologist to talk about dogma and apologetics. Pregnant with our first baby, starting her own small business, and wanting to have a conversation about a secular topic now and then, she didn't have the energy or the time to think about religion every second of every day, as I did. And she was very happy and content in her relationship with our Lord, desperately desiring a small church family to join and raise our family in.

I couldn't stop, though. I was intrigued and had to know more, but at each session, the teachings I learned from Sean became more painful because of what they meant should they be true. The Eucharist being the real Body and Blood of Christ? Mary and other saints able to intercede for me in prayer? Sean and I couldn't keep having religious debates in the middle of our sessions, either, and by this time I had resolved my personal issues and didn't need his professional service any longer.

We agreed, at my request, to keep discussing the teachings of the Catholic Church. He and his wonderful wife met me and Jessica at a Chinese restaurant. The Stevenses were foodies like us, so we had a lot to talk about. But Sean soon directed the con-versation to the real reason we had met that night: Catholicism. We broke out. Our wives watched. Sean kept his composure, and I kept my objections coming full swing. We were getting heated for sure.

He had just finished explaining the Immaculate Conception and the sinless soul of Mary when my wife squinted and piped up (for the first time in about twenty minutes): "I never saw it like that; that makes a lot of sense."

"See? I told you he was good," I said.

"Well, you don't make me feel that convincing!" Sean said, making us all laugh.

Sean handed me a copy of Scott and Kimberly Hahn's *Rome Sweet Home*, a book he had mentioned, and told me I could keep his personal copy. It wasn't the treatise I was expecting, but read-ing about and understanding the very personal struggle Hahn had in his conversion sincerely helped me in mine. As I read the book and considered the issues Hahn brings up, such as the Eucharist, the authority of the Church, and the role of the saints in our prayer, I became more convinced, and more questions circulated in my mind, but one thought surfaced that I could not dodge: "Can this be true? And if it is, it changes everything." With this enthusiasm, I told everyone about it.

My friends were curious, but I got the "That's what God is doing in *your* life, not mine" response. They meant well, but I realized quickly that I was alone. My wife, although supportive, asked me to promise her what Scott Hahn had promised his wife: to stop talking about it *all* the time! I complied.

Throughout a family Thanksgiving and Christmas, I discerned heavily just how important it *really* was to choose Catholicism. Was it completely necessary? Couldn't I remain a Protestant and still be a Christian? And what about my wife? She wasn't on the same page as I was at the time. Would I wait until she was? So many questions were surfacing that I wasn't sure where to turn.

One day I remembered that in *Rome Sweet Home*, the Hahns mention a book that they said helped bring them clarity about the Catholic Faith. So I scanned the book for the title, found that it was James Cardinal Gibbons's *Faith of Our Fathers*, and immediately ordered a copy. As soon as the book arrived, I started reading it and could not put it down. Every single page was so satisfyingly clear, charitable, and convincing. Cardinal Gibbons brilliantly begins simply, with God and the Trinity. From there he devotes one chapter to the final part of the Nicene Creed, which outlines the four marks of the Church: one (having unity), holy, catholic (universal), and apostolic (able to be traced back directly to the Apostles). After this, he explains the perpetuity of the Church, her infallible authority, and finally the relationship between the Church and the Bible.

After these chapters on the Church, I was convinced. More than just convinced, I didn't want to be a Christian any longer if I couldn't be Catholic. The framework of the Church is integral to the Body of Christ, Jesus Himself, and not a simple following or organization of like-minded people. If it is true of Jesus, it is true of the Church. I wanted to be part of His Body and nothing else.

After telling my wife and my family how I felt, I decided to contact my local parish to start RCIA. I was confirmed at the Easter Vigil in 2012. God brought me on a path I never could have foreseen and never would have believed.

Developing Your Testimony

Now that I've shared my story, let's look at how to develop and share your story with others. First, you need an outline. Your outline will include four elements: your theme, the details of why you're Catholic, your life after being a Catholic and the great benefits of your decision, and your offer to your listeners. My example included the first two elements. Let's look at each.

Find Your Theme

To begin creating an outline, choose a major theme. Many of us can relate to the common experiences of adolescence, marriage, kids, and the many joys of life. But there are also unavoidable trials—such as divorce, abuse, and miscarriage—to which many people can relate. Think of an event or experience that had an impact on your spiritual life, deepened your love for Jesus, or even led you to Jesus or to the Catholic Church as a convert.

Perhaps a conversion or a reversion might be your theme. Your story might contain something jarring that happened in your life, such as a near-death experience or an intellectual epiphany that connected the dots and gave your life meaning. Perhaps you have faced hardship or persecution for being a Christian or even thinking about being a Christian.

Often we overlook details about difficult experiences in our story and think that nobody would want to hear them or that we will embarrass ourselves by talking about them. Other times we prefer not to reopen old wounds. But God wants to use these experiences to reach others. Nobody is unfamiliar with difficult experiences, and therefore nobody is exempt from connecting with you when you share such experiences. If you have been hurt in the same way as someone else, you are able to relate to him deeply and personally.

Here is an example of a situation that opened the door to a closer relationship with one of my coworkers, about whom I knew little. During suicide awareness and prevention training at my workplace, this coworker piped up and explained that the problem of suicide was more than empty statistics on a Power-Point presentation, that it affects people in ways that others couldn't guess. She shared with us the story of how her mother committed suicide. Up until then I had thought this woman had it all. I had thought that everything in her life was perfect. Little did I know that this was something she probably brought with her everywhere, every night, and every holiday. Through my coworker's story, I was able to relate to her more fully, having had some suicidal issues of my own as a teen and having had friends who took their lives. Suicide is certainly not something to be glad about, but I was glad that she shared her story because from that point on, I have been better able to appreciate and understand her and her sensitivities.

That's the sort of thing that goes into your testimony. You don't have to reveal all your family secrets. By all means, maintain your privacy and appropriate boundaries, but don't be afraid to include things that help people relate to you as a fellow human being in our common journey of life.

Revealing these parts of your unique spiritual journey displays a side of you to others that will help them see you in a new frame of mind and listen to you differently. At first they might wonder, "Who is this holier-than-thou Christian who is trying to make me just like him?" or "He thinks he's so good!" But once you point out that you too are simply flesh and blood, you'll gain listeners. Few people turn away a good story, and although you aren't telling it for entertainment, you are telling it to make a case in a compelling fashion.

I want to clarify, though, that your testimony doesn't have to be based on a difficult or flabbergasting experience. All people of God have a unique story to tell. For example, if you're a cradle

Catholic and think you have had a rather uneventful spiritual journey, you still might have a strong faith and have reasons for keeping that faith. Tell people about why you hold on to the hope that is in you, why you're obedient to the Church's teaching, and what has helped you grow and maintain your faith for so long. Even if you've been Catholic your whole life, chances are good that there was a time when you decided to become a more serious and devout Catholic. Tell *that* story!

Develop the "Why I Am Catholic" Details

Next, develop the details about *why* you are a Catholic. These details are what helped you come to the Faith and grow in it. It might have been a struggle with the Eucharist and a conversation that turned the light on for you. Or it could have been a gesture from a complete stranger that made Catholics (or Christians in general) look attractive to you. You might even be a lifelong Catholic who has always had a deep sense of spiritual devotion. The idea is that you ought to develop the *reasons* you believe what you believe and how you can help others to take the same journey. Anecdotes such as these are useful to include, as they will serve as compelling reasons for others to consider becoming more serious about their faith, getting back to the practice of the Catholic Faith, or even converting. Give these big reasons embellished with smaller stories that highlight the bigger moments along your conversion timeline.

For example, if you're a convert, perhaps you and your neighbor broke out in a verbal joust over a statue of the Virgin Mary on his lawn that you were tired of looking at it. You might want to share how during that conversation you learned a few things about how Catholics revere the Blessed Virgin. And although it did not change your mind at the time, it did get you thinking. If you're a lifelong Catholic, you might begin with what motivates you to pray or with special occasions on your spiritual journey, and you should especially convey how your life with God is one of joy, peace, and security.

In discussing details in your testimony, avoid becoming a professor. That is, do *not* give the *Summa Theologica* of testimonies or even the CliffsNotes version. Your story should be personal and understandable, not scholarly. You are not telling your story to teach the "what" of your conversion but to highlight the fact that you came to an understanding or a turning point. You stand a good chance of losing your listeners if you fall into a deep discussion about Church teaching. Furthermore, if you remove the factual details of the issues you struggled with and simply say, "I came to understand this better," you will leave your listeners curious, and you will leave yourself open to answer their questions when you've finished. And yes, you should welcome the questions even if you feel unequipped.

Describe Your Life as a Catholic

Make sure you spend ample time discussing your life *as* a Catholic. Up until now, you might have your audience hanging on your words. You have described how you were unsatisfied with your life or how you went through some dramatic changes, and how you decided to continue following the Lord and trusting Jesus. Those changes took a toll on you, but was there sunshine in the end? Was it worth it? You might think so, but you had better convince your audience! As with selling a product or a service (I'm not watering down the gospel to a consumable good!), your goal is to inspire your listeners to deepen their faith or convert. If you don't convince them that you are satisfied with your results, why would they ever join you in following Christ or in following Him more faithfully? Think of it like this: if, at a job fair, you sensed that the interviewers didn't like the company they were working for, would you want the job with that company? Probably not, and if you neglect to tout the benefits of being Catholic, your audience will think the same when you share your testimony with them.

Go forward with confidence as you tell your *after* story. Tell your listeners of the wonderful community you belong to. Tell them of the amazing weight that was lifted when you first confessed to a priest even though you had been scared of judgment and condemnation. Share with them the confidence you have in the Church that has outlasted entire nations and their armies — that truly, the gates of Hades have not prevailed against her (Matt. 16:18). Explain to your listeners that they will find true and lasting riches like the ones you've found. And these "riches" can be whatever they are for you. Each person comes to the Church for different reasons and under different circumstances and experiences different joys and triumphs.

Make the Offer

The last ingredient in your testimony is the offer. Invite your listeners to share the experience you have been relating to them in your story. Ultimately, you are telling your story to encourage someone else to take that step toward conversion. You could leave your audience thinking, "Oh, that's all nice and interesting," but you need to aim for "I can do the same!"

Don't just offer the Faith to your listeners, but challenge them to seek for themselves. Leave them with a final thought that will keep them hungry for more. You could say something like this: "You know, I never thought I would become a Catholic, but I told myself I would give it a fair hearing. So, my friends, I urge you not to take my word for it but go read the Church Fathers and pick up books that outline what the early Church was all about." That sort of offer always gets some positive responses.

Another note on which to end your story is the "if you're ready" line. This gets everyone going. Everyone wants to feel up to the task, and since by now you have cultivated your audience's interest and curiosity, you need to plant the challenge in their minds. Tell them, "You might not be ready, but if you think you are up to it, look for yourself. What do you have to lose?" Saying, "You might not be ready" has the effect of motivating people to prove that they *are* ready. Then, even though they are attempting to prove you wrong, they are still looking and seeking and perhaps gaining new insights in the process.

Try challenging your listeners to delve into the patristic history of the Church; it's a powerful challenge to use. When people honestly seek the truth in Church history, they find that the Church has the same structure and beliefs today as she did two thousand years ago. It's a big selling point, so use it! People like consistency and steadfastness.

With all that in mind, there is something you need to avoid as well. Whatever you do, don't say anything that will put your audience off in the challenge you make to them. Avoid saying, for instance, "I dare you to find some Protestant teachings in the early Church, because if you do, you aren't being honest." Such negativity repels people and might discourage them from ever being open to the Church and her teachings.

Practice Sharing Your Testimony

Is there any more important part of a speech than the rehearsal? In giving your testimony, your confidence will rest entirely on your preparation.

It might be helpful to write out your testimonial outline and practice what you want to say. Mix things up, and see what works. You might not tell every detail in the order it happened, and you might decide you are dulling down the discussion with details that don't matter. Nip here and tuck there while working with your testimony, and jot down what works for you and for your audience. Hit those topics and stick to your plan!

After getting it on paper, rehearse! Repeat this as many times as needed and in different ways. Grab a stool and practice while seated. Rehearse it another time while standing in one spot. Try it in the shower. You've got to be comfortable giving your testimony in whatever situation the opportunity to do so arises. This ultimately defeats the "now isn't the right time" excuse (which I will discuss later).

Try rehearsing while your family or friends (I use my wife and my toddler) are in the room to act as potential distractions as you go through your presentation. This is an enormous help. If you can be sure of anything, it's the unexpected! You might ask them not to pay attention to you, but seek their attention. That will prepare you for times when someone in your audience looks as if he isn't interested (and it might bug you). Get your recording device out and film yourself. You are your own worst critic, so have multiple takes and figure out what you don't like. Show it to your spouse or a friend and ask for a critique. You might find that something you do is really distracting—something that you would never have thought of or that would never have caught your attention.

Brush up on public-speaking skills. I have laid out some of the essentials, but here are the big ones: stand still, don't say *um*, speak slowly and thoughtfully, use pauses, have a glass of water ready (if your speech is planned), and smile. Show that you are prepared. Show that you want to share your message (if you aren't interested in your message, your listeners won't be either). This will work for you!

Keep in mind as you develop your testimony what it is *not*. It is not a lecture. It is not a theological thesis or an explanation given at a seminar. Remember, don't base your discussion on *why* you believe what you believe. Instead, tell your audience simply *that* you came to believe it. If you begin explaining doctrines, some people will disagree with you, and once they trip on something they interpret differently, you will lose them. Keep their attention by moving through your story, not pausing to explain the nitty-gritty. The *only* thing you need to convince them of is that you were changed by Christ.

How Long Your Testimony Should Be

Recall that Peter tells us, "Always be prepared to make a defense to any one who calls you to account for the hope that is in you" (1 Pet. 3:15). You will have many opportunities to share your faith with believers and nonbelievers alike, and in different situations and settings. You might speak at an RCIA event or meet a stranger on a train and find that the topic comes up. You might be prepared in advance, or you might not. Think about and learn when to give the entire story and when to give the snapshot. Following is an example of each.

After I had become Catholic, my boss called me into his office. I sat down, and he sprang the question on me, "So, why Catholic?" Pause. I was caught off guard! This is a moment when you have to decide whether to make an apologetic response or not (*apologetics* being defense of the Faith). I can't give you the perfect formula for each and every possible situation, but in a case like this, unless someone objects, I would simply offer the broader part of my testimony. My answer: "Sir, you see, I didn't think it was for me, but I met a man who told me some pretty challenging stuff about Catholics. I didn't want to hear it and I didn't want to be Catholic, but after I had done some reading and verified his claims, it all started to make sense, and I knew I was in the wrong on several issues." I went on from there and wrapped it up.

This is your elevator speech; have it in your "back pocket" for such moments. This is where the rehearsal is critical, so choose your words carefully. I have a bad habit of overthinking things on the fly. If you have the same problem, slow down, think, and communicate a simple and honest testimony.

Other occasions will require you to give a much lengthier testimony. I remember from my days of going to Southern Baptist churches that every now and then the pastor would not give a message; instead, it would be open-mike testimony day. This was exciting. Anyone who had the guts or was inspired to speak did so. I know this sort of thing doesn't happen during Mass, but at an RCIA class or in another setting, you might have a similar opportunity.

Suppose your pastor invites you to give your testimony at a women's retreat. He explains that you will speak at x time and will have y number of minutes to tell your testimony. This is a huge favor he is doing you. You were handpicked to inspire others through your moving story, so prepare. Get that outline done, get a watch, and practice in the ways I mentioned earlier.

I just gave examples of two very different situations. To be prepared for various circumstances, consider forming three specific testimonies: one thirty seconds long, one three minutes long, and one five minutes long. The thirty-second speech will be your business pitch — your elevator speech — such as the reply

I gave to my boss in my earlier example. Make it quick for one of the on-the-go seeds you sow. Perhaps someone sees and asks about your crucifix while in the locker room. There might not be a lot of time to explain, but you can spread some gospel truth and food for thought in thirty seconds.

The three-minute and five-minute testimonies will require more detail and practice. I suggest that you use mental cues to help you remember what you want to talk about. There are two good ways to do this: a "point" or "bullet" outline and an acronym. For instance, you can prepare three points or five points in your testimony and spend a minute on each point. Or you can also come up with an acronym and spend a specific time on each letter.

As an example of mine, I use ABU, the name of the monkey in *Aladdin*. First, I explain the convincing use of apostolic succession (for A) in carrying our teachings like a baton through the ages. The Body (for B) is next, in which I express the Bible's emphasis on the reality of the Body of Christ. Lastly, I talk about the need for unity (for U) in the Church. My testimonial niche is more intellectual, so I spend time discussing these points in my three-minute testimony.

Of course, that is an example of a response to "Why did you decide to be Catholic?", but you should understand the use of the acronym. Its purpose is to create for you a mental reminder, however constructed, that works for you. This sort of preparation will give you a tremendous boost of confidence when you are given the opportunity to share your faith.

Now Share Your Story

After your testimony has been organized perfectly and the rehearsals have drilled it into your head, you need to do only two things: share and refresh. You didn't go through all the work and preparation for no reason. You desire to be an apostle of Jesus Christ, so now you need to take your testimony to the world. Have confidence in your hard work and the care you put into this task. Armed with the organizational plan I have outlined and your time spent practicing, you can be better prepared than you ever imagined. It might be nerve-racking, but sharing your testimony can really make a change in someone's life, so go and do your best!

Remember, people *want* to listen to you. Even if they don't understand, they still want the hope and joy you can bring them. The earth will not shake, and you probably won't have a burning-bush experience, but you are responsible for planting the seeds and cultivating the little plants others have started.

Refresh your memory and refresh your testimony periodically. In five or ten years, perhaps sooner, your story will have changed a little here and there, or dramatically elsewhere. Adjust your testimony to include the changes in your life, big or small. Every now and then, practice in the shower, while mowing the lawn, or wherever you please. Stay refreshed in your cues, and focus on what God is doing *now* in your life.

When you're faced with an opportunity to share your faith, don't think, "Now isn't the right time." Don't give in to the excuses your mind invents or to the excuses the devil proposes (after all, he does not want you to succeed). You might think you are unqualified, but you are a child of God! If anyone can speak on behalf of the Father, it is His children, so have confidence in your identity and not in your self-portrait.

Moses thought he was unqualified when God asked him to speak to Pharaoh.

But Moses said to God, "Who am I that I should go to Pharaoh, and bring the sons of Israel out of Egypt?" He said, "But I will be with you." (Exod. 3:11–12)

Moses then followed up with another excuse: "But ..." He did that four more times, and each time God showed Moses how He would intercede.

You might think you're a bad speaker. Reality check: everyone gets nervous. Moses gave this excuse too. God didn't deny that Moses had difficulty with speaking skills, nor did He change His plan to use Moses as His spokesman. God will give you the words; *trust in Him.*

Reflect briefly on the first Pentecost, when the disciples' mouths were opened and they were suddenly able to evangelize successfully. These were simple, uneducated men. Yet their testimonies converted an entire world! Let the Holy Spirit give you the words when you need them.

Maybe you just don't want to. But remember, you might provide someone's only chance to hear a moving story about the real life-changing power of Christ. Nothing is more powerful than a testimony. You are you, and no one knows your story better than you—so tell it!

There are so many other excuses and reasons you might have for not using your testimony, but have faith. Perhaps you have been led to Christ by someone's testimony; you will certainly want to give that gift to someone else. Remember all of these things, review them, and pray the following prayer:

Father, I know I am undeserving of the gift You have given me, but I pray for the sake of the Kingdom that You would please give me the words needed to change lives. Holy Spirit, please help me to be a messenger of the Gospel, and please speak to others through me. Amen.

3

Read the Bible Regularly

Ignorance of Scripture is ignorance of Christ.

—St. Jerome

I found one of the great loves of my life — the reading of Sacred Scripture — early on in my journey as a Christian. The stories of Moses and the Israelites, the wisdom of the prophets and the proverbs, and the story of Jesus and the rise of His Church witnessed in Acts and the epistles have all become a great treasure in my heart.

St. Jerome tells us, "Ignorance of Scripture is ignorance of Christ." This is why Scripture is woven throughout the Mass. Each Sunday we hear an Old Testament reading or a reading from the Acts of the Apostles, an excerpt from a psalm, a reading from a letter in the New Testament, and a reading from one of the four Gospels, all of which highlight some story in salvation history, "connecting the dots." These readings are chosen by the Church, not by an individual pastor, for those in every Catholic church to hear. And we do more than hear these words of Scripture: to the Old Testament and New Testament readings, we respond, "Thanks be to God"; we participate in the psalm by reciting the response; before the Gospel, we trace a tiny cross on our foreheads, our lips, and our hearts as a reminder to keep the Gospel words in our minds, on our lips, and in our hearts; and after the Gospel reading, during which we stand out of respect, we praise God for the wonderful words of encouragement and hope, saying, "Praise to you, Lord Jesus Christ." That's only the readings. The rest of the Mass is bathed in references to Scripture. The Mass is an encounter with God, a conversation in which we hear His words and respond with ours in prayer.

On the other six days of the week, though, when we Catholics aren't holding missals in our hands, there is a tremendous opportunity to keep the flame lit by reading the Bible each day at home.

We Catholics should be grateful to have the Church's Magisterium to help us and guide us in understanding the mysteries of the Bible. And although there is an immense amount of accumulated wisdom and teaching in the Church, you don't have to learn it all, or learn it all right away. The goal is not simply to learn things but to grow in faith and in love for God.

In case you don't already read and study Scripture regularly, this chapter will provide you with what you need to start: how to choose the Bible version that is right for you; how to read the Bible; basic tools for research and organization that will help you put Scripture to full use; and a tool that is sure to help you in time of need.

Choosing the Right Version

First, let's find the Bible that's right for you. There are a number of translations available that have been approved by the Church. Before the 1983 Code of Canon Law, any Apostolic See or ordinary within a diocese could approve a translation. That changed with the inclusion of canon 825, §1, which entrusts the Apostolic See and the episcopal conferences with the authority to approve translations.

Why different translations? Imagine reading a direct translation of Hebrew, word for word (a literal translation) versus a translation that is considerate of our grammatical nuances (a dynamic translation). One would be far more difficult to read and understand than the other. Moreover, some translations are easier to read without missing any of the context and meaning (a layman's translation). Therefore, some translations are meant to equip the scholar, while others are meant for more universal use, and others are meant to be easier to read.

The United States Catholic Conference of Bishops (USCCB) has approved fourteen translations since 1983, some of which are only the New Testament and some of which are only the Psalms. The most popular Catholic versions before and after 1983 are the ones I will discuss here, hoping to help you find a new or more suitable Bible for your needs.

• *Douay-Rheims.* I will start with the standard translation for English-speaking Catholics until the 1960s, the Douay-Rheims (D-R) Bible. This is a wonderful translation whose historical significance cannot be overstated, although I don't have the space to write about that. Although the language is archaic, those older words and statements seem more powerful and inspiring than the way we speak today; "Thou shalt" strikes us with authority more than today's "You must." But even Catholics who prefer a more modern translation can still use the Douay-Rheims for occasional reference.

• *New American Bible (NAB).* This is the most widely used Catholic Bible in the United States, largely due to the fact that it was produced by the USCCB and the Catholic Bible Association and because it is the translation that is used for Mass readings. It is a literal translation, but having been updated a number of times since the 1950s, it reads very well (although the Old Testament reads slightly differently from the New). Despite its popularity, the NAB is not considered a good Bible for study and has a limited selection of study materials available for it.

• *Revised Standard Version Catholic Edition (RSVCE)*. For its accuracy, ease, and readability, the RSVCE has been the leading choice for scholars for most of the twentieth century and to the present. It is a very literal translation but is preferred by many. Because the RSVCE is still a top choice for scholars, many study tools are available for it. I recommend the *Ignatius Study Bible*, which is sold in separate New and Old Testament versions and is jam-packed with information to help you understand Scripture better.

• *New Revised Standard Version Catholic Edition (NRSVCE)*. This Bible was the product of a collaboration of Catholic, Orthodox, and Protestant scholars who wanted to develop an accurate, but less literal version of the RSVCE. For many, the NRSVCE is the scholar's standard and is required for many seminarians. It incorporates modern discoveries such as the Dead Sea Scrolls and the apocrypha, which are the books that were not selected to be included in the Bible by the primitive Church. As one would expect, this version has a plethora of study tools available for it, perhaps the most. These include interlinear Bibles, which show the new translation and the original language side by side on the same page, concordances (which I describe late in this chapter), and dictionaries and commentaries that bring the words into context and meaning.

• *New Jerusalem Bible (NJB)*. The New Jerusalem Bible is a "dynamic equivalence" translation; the translation's effect on its reader is meant to be roughly the same as the effect of the source text on its source reader. This makes the NJB a readable and accurate translation. A common touch that many notice is the direct use of the divine name YHWH (Yahweh) instead of LORD, which is found in just about any other translation. The humble use of inclusive language gives this translation a special feel, and many readers appreciate the poetic sections, such as the Psalms and the Song of Solomon. The NJB's only drawback is the lack of available study tools for it. There are common study tools to help you get the most out of your Bible, but not a wide selection.

How to Read the Bible (and More)

It would be easy to tell you just to buy a Bible, open up to Matthew's Gospel, and get started. That's a quick way to get bored and not pick the Bible up again. Instead you need a plan. A plan will give you a start, a goal, and how to get there. There are many ways to read Scripture. Here are just three ways to use your Bible regularly that will give you confidence and satisfaction.

• *Along with the Mass.* A good way to begin reading the Bible is to follow along with the daily Mass readings, which will also serve to unite you further with Catholics throughout the world, who hear the same readings at Mass. Catholics are all on the same page, literally.

Daily Mass readings can easily be found online with any search engine. The USCCB website (www.usccb.org) offers easy access to the daily readings for the entire liturgical year as well as reflections from some of today's top Catholic thinkers. If you're into electronic devices, there are numerous apps (some are free) that contain this information. A couple of the best are Laudate and iMissal.

The missalettes in your parish church list daily Mass readings. You may also subscribe to monthly publications such as *Magnificat* and *God's Word*, which include all the Mass readings, along with thoughtful prayer intentions, reflections, articles, daily devotions, and advertisements for popular resources to help you grow in spirit and truth.

• *Lectio continua* is Latin for "continuous reading." This form of Bible reading is like reading any book: you read a section at one time, and the next time you read, you pick up where you left off. A distinction needs to be made, however. Scripture is not fiction. It is the very Word of God! Although lectio continua may seem like ordinary reading, it is a systematic way of reading God's Word. When you read Scripture in continuation, you understand the big picture and are then able to understand the smaller nuggets of teaching within.

Lectio continua does not mean reading from Genesis to Revelation in one pass. That's a recipe for disaster, because once you get to Leviticus and Deuteronomy and Numbers, books that are filled with Levitical Law and census information, it's easy to get bored and quit. Those books are best taken up with study material to show their significance. Rather, in lectio continua, *you* choose where to start and which passages you will continually read.

I find lectio continua to be a very meaningful way to read the Bible, especially the more narrative books, such as Genesis, Exodus, and the Gospels—with stories such as those of Joseph coming to terms with his brothers who had sold him as a slave out of jealousy; of Moses taking on Pharaoh; of twelve ordinary men selected for an extraordinary journey as Apostles. The foundations of salvation history are found in the opening books of the Bible. Others, such as the Psalms and the wisdom books of Proverbs, Ecclesiastes, and Wisdom, contain beautiful prayers and a wealth of spiritual direction that we can apply right here, right now, in our daily lives.

If you choose to read the Bible in this way, I suggest that you devise a plan. Outline your objective: Do you want to read through an entire Gospel, an epistle, or the entire Old Testament? How many pages or chapters can you read in one sitting? How many days a week can you devote to reading? How much time per day can you commit to? I suggest about fifteen minutes per day as a fair place to start. Then commit! Commit to reading exactly what you've determined to be doable; don't bite off more than you can chew.

Additionally, I suggest that you find another person to pledge to follow a similar schedule, so that you can hold each other accountable and discuss the readings together. This might be your spouse, a parent, a friend, your roommate; choose someone who can keep you motivated to read along.

Another suggestion is to journal your thoughts and meditations. I consider thoughts and meditations the same in lectio continua, but the meditation will become more pronounced in a form of reading called *lectio divina*, which I will get to next. In your journal, simply make a small entry about what you read, what you think about it, and how it applies to you. This will help you to memorize passages of the Bible and remember teachings and will allow the spiritual dimension of these mysteries to sink in.

• *Lectio divina.* Reading in the form of lectio continua has a sense of pace, narration, and story reading. Another form of

Bible reading brings us down a gear, slows our mind, and helps us focus on a specific portion of Scripture in prayer. This is known as *lectio divina*, which means "divine reading." It is a powerful form of reading that brings Scripture into our head, our heart, and our spirit. Lectio divina is an ancient tool that Catholics have preserved through Benedictine monks and is now widely used even among the laity. This, I believe, is what the Council Fathers had in mind when they mentioned, "While invoking the Holy Spirit, they seek in these very Scriptures God as it were speaking to them in Christ."[5]

Lectio divina has four main parts: *lectio*, *meditatio*, *oratio*, and *contemplatio*. Let's look at each.

Lectio is the part in which Scripture is not just read, but is also listened to. We have all had the experience of reading a paragraph, being interrupted by a thought, and finding ourselves at the end of the paragraph without knowing what we've read. In lectio divina we focus on what we are reading with intent and expectation. As we read slowly and attentively, we listen for the gentle murmuring of God's message to us, the "still small voice" touching our hearts (see 1 Kings 19:12).

Meditatio. The ancient meaning of meditating on Scripture has a funny explanation. You might not guess that to meditate on Scripture means to "ruminate" on it—to chew or gnaw on it slowly, like an animal chewing its cud. Our parents told us to chew our food thoroughly so that our bodies could better extract and process its nutrients. In the same way, we benefit more from ruminating on

---

[5] *Unitatis Redintegratio*, no. 21.

God's Word than by merely reading it. When we meditate on Scripture we ponder its truths in our hearts, as Mary pondered the events of Christ's life and kept them in her heart (cf. Luke 2:19, 51).

Oratio (prayer). In this stage, inspired by our reading and meditation on God's Word, we speak to God from our hearts.

Contemplatio. In contemplation we sit in a state of mental relaxation and quietness, a silence that allows our hearts and minds to consider the meaning and effect of the whole lectio divina. The contemplation is simply our opportunity to sit for five to fifteen minutes (or longer) and enjoy the silence of listening to God.

Lectio divina can be used in private or in a group setting. If you use it on your own, set aside a certain time when you will not be disturbed or disrupted—just you, your Bible, and maybe a notepad. If you plan to use lectio divina in a group, which I highly suggest, it helps to have somebody prepare a relevant piece of Scripture for the group to meditate on, and then individuals can share their insights when the four steps of lectio divina are finished. Lectio divina is particularly strong in bringing together married couples in prayer, specifically because of the *oratio*, in which the spouses dedicate and consecrate themselves to the Lord, forming what I call the marriage Trinity: the husband, the wife, and God.

I have provided three meaningful ways in which you can deepen your love of Scripture. There are many other ways to study Sacred Scripture, and perhaps you'll find a technique that helps you better, but these three proven techniques are a good place to start.

Filling Our Father's House

Bible Tools

Following are some tools that can help you understand Scripture better.

• *Concordance.* There are over thirty thousand verses and over eighty thousand words in the Bible. If you want to find a certain verse based on a word search, you could use a concordance. There are a number of uses for this tool, and I have found myself using it far more than I would have expected, but I am lucky and married a woman who happened to own a few.

For example, if I wanted to find all the verses that contained the word *church*, I would look up the word in the alphabetical list in a concordance and find a reference that looks like this:

CHURCH See also CHURCHES
Mt 16:18   upon this rock I will build my **c.**   1577
Mt 18:17   tell it unto the **c.**   1577
Mt 18:17   but if he neglects to hear the **c.**   1577
Ac 2:47   the Lord added to the **c.** daily   1577

And so on. The concordance lists the locations of the word by book, in their order in the Bible, and then by chapter and verse. Next, the word is in bold, abbreviated, with its contextual words on either side. In my example, if I remembered that the Bible contains a verse in which Jesus explicitly speaks of the foundation of His Church, but I couldn't remember which book or chapter the verse was in, I could pull out my concordance and find it. Further, if I wanted to see all the uses of any word in the Bible, I could do so with this tool.

Lastly, there is a number (above, 1577) following the location and word context. This is the number that the concordance assigns the individual word, and it tells you where to find that word in the dictionary in the back of the concordance. So, if I wanted to find the meaning of the word *church* in Matthew 16:18, I would go to its number in the concordance dictionary and find the definition and the original word in Greek (or in another original language). A good concordance is a great word-search tool and doubles as a dictionary.

Many study Bibles include a small concordance and perhaps a dictionary too. These are great tools and list the page numbers of words, which makes them easy to find. However, these smaller concordances are usually only keywords. A complete concordance is concerned with *every* word and is thus exhaustive in its use. It is a must-have for the serious student of Scripture, for anyone who develops Bible studies, and for anyone who wants to explore Scripture further.

• *Language tools and software.* Sometimes understanding Scripture requires a certain understanding of the original language it was written in and of the language certain parts would have been spoken in. For example, Protestants often misinterpret the language in Matthew 16:18, "I tell you, you are Peter ['rock'], and on this rock I will build my church." They reason that since the original Greek used two different words for "rock," *petros* for Peter and *petras* for the foundation of Jesus' Church, Jesus was not talking about building His Church on Peter. Jesus spoke Aramaic, however, and would have used *Kepa* for Peter and *kepa* for the foundation of the Church. The Greek uses a masculine and a feminine pronoun. Further, Jesus and the Gospel writer observed certain grammar rules, such as, in this case, that one cannot use two masculine pronouns or two feminine pronouns in a sentence, so it would make grammatical sense for Jesus to use a masculine pronoun to refer to Peter. Understanding these rules is what unlocks the finer meanings of Scripture.

The meaning of many parts of Scripture can be clarified with a proper understanding of the original language, but you don't have to have a degree or formal education to attain the benefits of good linguistic scholarship. You can gain those benefits through the use of certain language software and websites. There are a number of available programs and websites, but I will highlight two, neither of which I am being paid to tell you about.

Blue Letter Bible (BLB; www.blueletterbible.org) is a website that contains the whole Bible and hyperlinks each word to several available tools. At BLB you can find a word in its original language, its definition, available commentaries on its uses throughout the Bible through a complete concordance, audio pronunciation, and more. I use this source almost constantly because it's free, exhaustive, easy to use, and convenient.

Verbum from Logos Bible Software is, I think, the future of exegetical Scripture study software. It is an all-in-one package that makes Scripture study a cinch, and it is distinctively Catholic. When you search a word or select a work from a reading, Verbum points you to a long list of references, resources, and Church documents that discuss that selection and enhance your understanding of it. Logos Verbum is not a free service, but it offers a world of information that you can have at your fingertips. There are different levels of Logos software packages that are endorsed by several Catholic personalities, such as Scott Hahn, Jeff Cavins, Mike Aquilina, Jimmy Akin, Steve Ray, and Patrick Madrid.

Read the Bible Regularly

Although Bible software benefits the student of Scripture in many ways, not every Bible-reading Catholic needs or even wants to venture into this level of learning. Understand your needs and goals and continue from there.

Scripture Memorization

Each day we all work from two deposits of information: just-in-case information and just-in-time information. Just-in-case information includes items such as your social security number, your blood type, or your niece's favorite superhero. This sort of information is used, as its name indicates, just in case you need to remember it on occasion. Whether such occasions come up often or not, just in case you need the information, you have it in a mental zip drive.

Just-in-time information could be the number on your cockpit preflight checklist, the answers for a test, or instructions on how to get to the mall. This information comes in handy just in time for its use and might never be used again, or it's so simple that you never forget it. In any case, you'll want to know where to find such information. You might want to memorize it, or you might not.

Scripture could fall into either category. Lengthy passages would fall into the just-in-time category because you wouldn't memorize entire chapters but would memorize their location. For example: you should always know the location of such important passages as the Creation accounts (Gen. 1—2), Noah and the Flood (Gen. 6), the Ten Commandments (Exod. 20), the Sermon on the Mount (Matt. 5—7), the parable of the prodigal son (Luke 15), and so forth. On the other hand, in the case of Scripture that falls into the just-in-case category, there are specific verses that you *do* want to memorize. For example, should you need to remind yourself that you are God's friend, you'll want to know John 15:15; or that God will provide a way out in times of temptation, you'd memorize 1 Corinthians 10:13; or when you need to be an apologist you'd do well to memorize verses such as John 6:51 for the Eucharist, 1 Peter 3:15 to defend the Faith, 2 Timothy 3:16 for the proper use of Scripture and 1 Timothy 3:15 to defend the Church as the pillar and foundation of truth.

In today's busy and information-flooded world, it can be very difficult to memorize things—especially the passwords galore we're expected to remember. And with information at our fingertips, maybe we've lost the art of memorization—at least for useful information. For instance, I can't tell you what my driver's license number is, but I can recite with precision the names and numbers of the University of North Dakota men's hockey team each year, their individual approximate weight, and probably their stats throughout the year. I'm that into it.

Memorization can be a useful skill, though, and what better material for it than Scripture! Memorizing Scripture is not only a good mental exercise but is also conducive to prayer (if, for instance, you have memorized psalms or parts of psalms), helpful in fighting temptation and growing in holiness (if, before you say something in anger, you recall St. James's powerful reminder to bridle your tongue [James 3:5–6]), comforting (if, in your anxiety, you reflect on Christ's words about God's providence [Matt. 6:25–33]), and, of course, essential for defending the Faith on the spot. In all these instances, having a Scripture passage in your head or on the tip of your tongue comes in very handy.

Amid the busyness of your life, though, how is it possible to memorize Scripture? As you start to orient your mind toward memorizing some Scripture, remember these key points:

- Take it slow. You don't need to memorize a lot. A few key verses are enough to get started.

- You can remember the location or the words, but always remember the use and the association.

- Don't let verse memory replace your regular reading of Scripture. God's Word is the spiritual food that will nourish your soul. Sometimes you need a snack, but you can't go without the meal.

- Commit! Some verses are just in case, some are just in time. You are memorizing, though, so be in it for the long haul.

Okay, let's get started. How do you memorize Scripture? There are three components to verse memory: relation, location, and association.

Relation refers to two things. One is why the particular Scripture verse is important to you. Are you using the specific verse for apologetics and for defense of the Faith? Are you trying to overcome a certain sin? Are you looking to be reminded of God's love for you? Relation also concerns context of the verse. Consider these questions when determining how to memorize a verse.

- What is the context of the verse you want to memorize?

- What category does it fall under (e.g., apologetics, sin, prophecy)?

- Is it a parable, a narration, or a statement?

- Was it spoken by someone? If so, by whom?

Each of these will put a frame of reference in your mind so that when you are reminded of the verse, you can put the puzzle pieces together. That's the first part of memorizing Scripture: remembering what the verse has to do with.

Location. A verse's location will serve you even if you don't remember its exact words. For example, if you want to read about the Creation narrative, you would go to the beginning of Genesis. That's an easy example, but it works the same for the rest of Scripture. If you know that there is something about the Eucharist in chapter 6 of John's Gospel, you can go there or point someone else in that direction. Or if you wanted to be more specific, you could remember that there are important words from Jesus regarding Church authority in Matthew 16:18 and 18:18. You don't have to know exactly what these verses say, but it helps to know where they are in the Bible in case you need to find them yourself or point someone else to their location.

Association is where you put relation and location to work in verse memory. The relation is how the information relates to your need and its context, and the location is where the verse is found in the Bible. In association, you connect the two; for example, Jesus discusses the Eucharist in John 6. There are over fifty verses in John 6, and you don't have them all memorized, but knowing that Jesus discusses the Eucharist in John 6 will let you point someone else to that chapter, or if you have a computer, a smartphone, or a Bible on hand, you can go right to it yourself.

Here are four common ways to practice association:

1. *Writing.* The more you write something, the better you remember it. Writing helps you think over your words so they sink in. So get a sheet of paper, or open a document on your computer, and write or type the association over and over: "Learn to defend the Faith

because Peter commands us to do so in 1 Peter 3:15."
Repeat.

2. *Begin talking about it.* Talk with your friends regularly
about these topics, and do your best to be "on the
spot." Again, do it over and over. Scripture is like a
language: you won't learn to use it unless you start
talking in that language.

3. *Sword drill.* Scripture is your sword. Have someone call
out a verse, and then open your Bible, find the verse,
and read it out loud. Do this with your favorite verses.
Over time you will quickly become closely acquainted
with the contents.

4. *Flash cards.* Do I have to explain? They work. Just take
five minutes a day and review them. That's it.

How can you use verse memorization to lead others to Christ
or to defend the Faith? You could tell someone that the Bible says
that there is a relationship between faith and works — it's not
all about one or the other — but it would be more convincing to
say, "Habakkuk 2:4 says, 'The righteous shall live by faith,' and
James 2:26 says, 'Faith apart from works is dead.' See, Scripture
in its whole contains a message of faith and works."

I have a saying: "When someone asks me what time it is,
I tell him how to build a watch." I have a bad habit of giving
too much information. There are times where too much information can put someone off, but too little information will
make you look ignorant. Knowing when to use information is
one thing, but when you've memorized some Scripture, you'll
always have information on hand that you'll need just in case
and just in time.

For further reading on Scripture memorization for apologetics or other uses, I strongly recommend Dr. Kevin Vost's *Memorize the Faith!* and *Memorize the Reasons!*

Suggested Sites, Authors, and Studies

Scott Hahn's St. Paul Center for Biblical Theology. Scott Hahn is one of the guys who inspired my generation of apologists, scholars, and converts in general. His Center for Biblical Theology is great for Catholics who are looking to dive into Sacred Scripture. On the center's website (www.salvationhistory.com), you can find numerous resources on Scripture, liturgy, apologetics, and more. The center can help *you* build a parish Bible study, or you can join its online studies on a variety of topics.

Elena Bosetti. A personal favorite for private study and reflection on Scripture is Elena Bosetti, a distinguished student and professor of New Testament studies. I was introduced to her works in my Sacred Scripture courses at Holy Apostles and thought I had a nice little secret. Turns out she is quite popular. Actually, "popular" is an understatement: Bosetti teaches at the Pontifical Gregorian University and at the Theological Institute of Consecrated Life in Rome, and also at the Institute of Religious Studies in Modena, Italy, and is a top-shelf author and instructor in Scripture. See her four books on the Gospels.

Here are a few more books I am confident you will find helpful:

The Bible Compass: A Catholic's Guide to Navigating the Scriptures by Edward Sri

The Great Adventure Catholic Bible Timeline by Jeff Cavins

Walking with God by Jeff Cavins

You Can Understand the Bible: A Practical and Illuminating Guide to Each Book in the Bible by Peter Kreeft

The Catholic Church and the Bible by Peter Stravinskas

Understanding the Scriptures: A Complete Course on Bible Study by Scott Hahn

A Father Who Keeps His Promises by Scott Hahn

Making Senses Out of Scripture by Mark Shea

St. John's Gospel by Steve Ray

For a look at the Bible from an apologetics perspective:

Memorize the Faith! by Dr. Kevin Vost

Where's That in the Bible? by Patrick Madrid

A Biblical Defense of the Catholic Church by Dave Armstrong

Handbook of Catholic Apologetics by Dr. Peter Kreeft and Ronald Tacelli

Because this chapter is dedicated to Sacred Scripture, it is also necessary to note a point on which Catholics and Protestants differ: the important relationship between Scripture and Tradition—that Scripture is *an* authority but not the *sole* authority. It would take me another book to expound on this topic, so I will leave you with suggestions for reading. I recommend that you start with *Dei Verbum*, Vatican II's Dogmatic Constitution on Divine Revelation. It is a quick 5,000-word read and can be found on the Vatican's website (www.vatican.va). On my website (www.shaunmcafee.com), you will find a concise summary of *Dei Verbum*'s contents as well as other Vatican II documents.

For further reading on Scripture and Tradition, see:

The Meaning of Tradition by Yves Congar, O.P.

Tradition and the Church by Msgr. George Agius, D.D., J.C.D.

Magisterium: Teacher and Guardian of Faith by Cardinal Avery Dulles, S.J.

Scripture and Tradition in the Church by Patrick Madrid

God's Word by Cardinal Joseph Ratzinger (Pope Benedict XVI)

I want to conclude this chapter with something very short and sweet adapted from the introduction to the *Ignatius Study Bible*:

You are approaching the "word of God". But for thousands of years, since before he knit you in your mother's womb, the Word of God has been approaching you.[6]

---

[6] Scott Hahn and Curtis Mitch, "Approaching the Sacred Scriptures," *Ignatius Insight*, http://www.ignatiusinsight.com/features2005/hahn_mitch_ss_aug05.asp.

4

Deepen Your Personal Relationship with Jesus

*The spiritual life, however, is not
limited solely to participation in the liturgy.
The Christian is indeed called to pray
with his brethren, but he must also enter into
his chamber to pray to the Father, in secret.*

—*Sacrosanctum Concilium*, no.12

The Lord calls us all to have a personal relationship with Him. This personal relationship is based on knowledge—God knowing us and we knowing God. God already knows us; His knowledge is perfect. Despite our best attempts to ignore Him, God has always known us. But we weren't born with this knowledge of God.

Even when we discover God through revelation, we might know *about* God but still might not *know* Him. In the Bible, to "know" someone is to engage in sexual intercourse with that person. When we speak of knowing God, and of God knowing us, we are speaking about a different but similarly intimate relationship with Him.

Jesus tells His disciples:

53

Not every one who says to me, "Lord, Lord," shall enter the kingdom of heaven, but he who does the will of my Father who is in heaven. On that day many will say to me, "Lord, Lord, did we not prophesy in your name, and cast out demons in your name, and do many mighty works in your name?" And then will I declare to them, "I never knew you; depart from me, you evildoers." (Matt. 7:21–23)

Paul tells the Christians in Galatia:

Formerly, when you did not know God, you were in bondage to beings that by nature are no gods; but now that you have come to know God, or rather to be known by God, how can you turn back again to the weak and beggarly elemental spirits, whose slaves you want to be once more? (Gal. 4:8–9)

It is clear that those who will be accepted into heaven are those who know God, who have a personal relationship with Him. The question is: What does it mean to have a personal relationship with the Lord? It means that we let God be in charge of our lives, that we form a relationship with His Mystical Body, and that we get to know His Mother. It also demands that we seek a constant and perpetual conversion, serve others in love, and create disciples.

Let's look at various ways to develop or deepen your personal relationship with the Lord: through prayer, letting God be in control of your life, being involved with the Church, growing in devotion to the Blessed Mother, and seeking spiritual direction.

Pray

Because prayer is personal, it is the most direct way of developing and maintaining a personal relationship with the Lord. The time we spend talking to our loved ones, and listening to their needs and concerns, allows our relationship with them to grow deeper. Likewise, when we grow in our relationship with God through prayer, we come to understand Him better and to understand His will for us.

A good prayer life requires practice, discipline, commitment, openness, honesty, and love. To get a good start on your prayer life, or even to add to it, look for a book of Catholic prayers, of which there are many kinds. Also, check out a breviary, which is a book of liturgical prayers. There are also several apps for your phone or tablet that contain many prayers, including the breviary. Make a place in your home, a room or a corner, for prayer.

To read more about developing a personal relationship with Jesus through prayer, see the following books.

The Three Ages of the Interior Life by Reginald Garrigou-Lagrange

Tending the Temple and *Through, With, and In Him* by Shane Kapler

Prayer for Beginners by Peter Kreeft

Prayer for Your Everyday Life, *Prayers of the Women Mystics*, and *A Mother's Treasury of Prayers* by Rhonda Chervin

Give God Control

In flight training, when one pilot hands the control over to the other, the receiver says, "My controls," and the giver responds with, "Your controls" as he lets go of all controls, and again the receiving pilot responds with "I have full control." When we have a personal relationship with Jesus, we aren't even copilots, because He is always in control. He never needs a break, never is overcome by fatigue, and is always attentive to our needs as He carries us through life. When we trust God and give Him complete control of our lives — which we never really had much control over in the first place — God performs maneuvers and makeovers that we never thought possible. Moreover, He removes all boundaries that hold us down and frees our spirits to soar.

This is especially true in the case of sin. We cannot become free of sin and distress until we let God transform us. We let God transform us by participating in the sacraments, serving others, praying, and reading Scripture regularly. When we allow God full control we will come to understand His will for us, we will trust Him more, and we will receive what we actually long for.

A Relationship with the Church

A personal relationship with Jesus also means a personal relationship with His Church. Recall the story of Saul on his way to Damascus to punish and persecute Christians.

> But Saul, still breathing threats and murder against the disciples of the Lord, went to the high priest and asked him for letters to the synagogues at Damascus, so that if he found any belonging to the Way, men or women, he might bring them bound to Jerusalem. Now as he journeyed he approached Damascus, and suddenly a light from heaven flashed about him. And he fell to the ground and heard a voice saying to him, "Saul, Saul, why do you persecute me?" And he said, "Who are you, Lord?" And he said, "I am Jesus, whom you are persecuting." (Acts 9:1–5)

Saul must have been confused. He persecuted Christians, this he knew, but the voice he heard was not one of the men or women he had directly persecuted. This voice was telling him that by persecuting Christ's people, Saul was persecuting Christ Himself. Saul, who later became Paul, would soon realize that Jesus identifies directly with His people — not in a symbolic way, but in reality.

Because of this identity, the Second Vatican Council document *Lumen Gentium* rightly says:

> God gathered together as one all those who in faith look upon Jesus as the author of salvation and the source of unity and peace, and established them as the Church that for each and all it may be the visible sacrament of this saving unity. (no. 9)

And also:

> Rising from the dead [Jesus] sent His life-giving spirit upon His disciples and through Him has established His Body which is the Church as the universal sacrament of salvation. (no. 48)

We see clearly that the Church is the most profound institution in the world. Jesus came to establish the kingdom of God, and to make that happen, He established a Church and promised to remain with her always (Matt. 28:20). He has given His Church authority (see Matt. 10:16; 28:19) and commissioned her to teach and to remind His people of everything He said (John 14:26; 16:13).

We are therefore called to have a relationship with Jesus *and* His Church. To have a good relationship with the Church, we should turn to her as a source of truth, participate in her sacraments, and obey her laws, for when we obey the Church, we obey Christ:

> He who hears you hears me, and he who rejects you rejects me, and he who rejects me rejects him who sent me. (Luke 10:16)

"Behold Your Mother"

If we love Jesus and wish to follow Him, it is natural for us to love His Mother, who is our Mother as well. Jesus Himself gave Mary to us all (John 19:27; Rev. 12:17).

We read the Gospels written by the Apostles but perhaps rarely consider the wisdom Mary has to offer as the one person who lived close to thirty years with Jesus. Mary was also the first disciple of Jesus, and in her we have a loving and nurturing example of what it is to petition Jesus: "They have no wine." And she urges us, "Do whatever he tells you" (John 2:3, 5).

Devotion to Mary includes talking to her in prayer, requesting that our petitions be granted through her intercession. We can also pray the Rosary, read about Mary and ponder her life, make St. Louis de Montfort's Consecration to Jesus through Mary,[7] and strive to imitate her, as she is the greatest disciple of Christ. In imitation of Mary, we are called to simplicity, meditation,

---

[7] This brilliant form of giving ourselves to Jesus through Mary was formed by St. Louis de Montfort of the early eighteenth century, a pious young man who became a priest in Paris after leaving everything behind to follow Christ. You can find information on St. Louis's Consecration online, and there are also free courses to lead you through this devotion at Holy Apostles College and Seminary's Massive Open Online Course (MOOC), which I've listed in the resources section of this book.

perseverance in suffering, and discipleship; we are also called to present Christ to the world. When we love Mary in these visible ways, we can be sure we are pleasing Jesus because, as one would expect, Jesus loves those who love His Mother.

For further reading on growing closer to Jesus through Mary, see Scott Hahn's *Hail, Holy Queen*, St. Louis de Montfort's *True Devotion to Mary*, and Pope John Paul II's *Theotokos: Woman, Mother, Disciple*.

Perpetual Conversion

Having a personal relationship with Christ means that we are called to ongoing conversion. It is a journey in which we continually grow in the Lord. We grow in many ways: we deepen our faith; we get to know the saints and the family of believers; we become more compassionate toward the poor and the hungry; we become better fathers and mothers.

Perpetual conversion calls for endurance. To face the flaming arrows of the enemy and the inevitable hardships in our lives, we must ask the Lord to pour out His Holy Spirit on us. And with the help of the Spirit, we must develop virtues and strive to overcome our vices. This will not happen overnight, though. We must gradually empty ourselves by practicing good habits. If we put a dirty dish into the sink and run water into it, eventually the contents of that dish will be only new, clean water. We need the same constant flow of God's grace into our lives in order to replace our vices with virtues: prayer, brotherly love, obedience, joy, peace, service to others, and humility.

Spiritual Direction

Another way to develop or deepen your relationship with the Lord is through spiritual direction. A spiritual director is a mentor—a priest or a layperson—who can help you discern and find your vocational direction and help you to hear God's voice. As a world-class player needs a personal trainer, each of us needs a dedicated person to help us find our way. St. Josemaría Escrivá de Balaguer puts it perfectly:

> You wouldn't think of building a good house to live in here on earth without an architect. How can you ever hope, without a director, to build the castle of your sanctification in order to live forever in heaven?[8]

My favorite example of a spiritual director/directee relationship is that of Paul and Timothy in the New Testament. Paul, as the older, experienced, educated, and vigilant apostle, was well equipped to serve and send the young and budding Timothy on his mission. Because Timothy wanted to be an apostle, he needed a mentor who had been down the road he would travel, someone who could relate to and understand the person he needed to become to finish the race.

A spiritual director is not the person to help you clean up your emotional and psychological issues. We all have messes, but your director is not a psychologist; he is there to offer insight on what the Lord is calling you to do in life. Your director will help you develop your prayer life and grow in holiness and will assist you with any difficulties you might experience in your spiritual life.

A good illustration of this is a swimmer who is attempting to cross a large body of choppy water, as we do in life. He swims according to the direction of his coach, who is on the shore, telling him when he is off course, when he needs to rest, and when he needs to refocus. The tricky thing is that the swimmer cannot

---

[8] St. Josemaría Escrivá de Balaguer, *The Way*, no. 60.

see above the waves even when he attempts to tread water; he has to trust his coach. However, if the coach is on a platform at the swimmer's destination, he is all the better equipped to make sure the swimmer makes the crossing successfully.

To be sure your coach is on a platform that will equip him to guide you successfully, you must find an adviser who is right for you. Choose a person of similar disposition, someone who shares your interests and philosophies. If you are more geared toward academics and theology, find someone who has a similar capacity and passion. If you lean toward missionary service abroad, find an adviser who has experience in that vocation. Find someone you trust, respect, and look up to. Above all, find someone who has an authentically Catholic faith, who has absolutely no disagreement with the Magisterium, whom you will not have to dance around issues with.

Get to Know Christ and See Him in Others

Your whole purpose in this world is to have a personal relationship with the Lord of the universe. Sounds pretty cool, right? It's true. The thing is, God already knows everything about you. The world will tell you that you need to discover who you are. What you really need to discover is the one who already knows who you are. When you align yourself with this Person, you will discover what you truly want, need, and are made to do.

Being a disciple of Christ means serving others. When we love our neighbors and serve the poor, we are serving Jesus Himself, who directly identifies with the struggles of the world. We are also called to have an intimate relationship with Jesus through the Church, which is His Mystical Body. Vatican II's *Gaudium et Spes* communicates the importance of the Church to the modern man:

That the earthly and the heavenly city penetrate each other is a fact accessible to faith alone; it remains a mystery of human history.... Pursuing the saving purpose which is proper to her, the Church does not only communicate divine life to men but in some way casts the reflected light of that life over the entire earth, most of all by its healing and elevating impact on the dignity of the person, by the way in which it strengthens the seams of human society and imbues the everyday activity of men with a deeper meaning and importance. Thus through her individual matters and her whole community, the Church believes she can contribute greatly toward making the family of man and its history more human. (no. 40)

If you're looking for more reading material on developing a personal relationship with Jesus, I suggest the following:

The Three Ages of the Interior Life by Reginald Garrigou-Lagrange

Sermons of the Church Fathers

Introduction to the Devout Life by St. Francis de Sales

The Story of a Soul by St. Thérèse of Lisieux

The Way of Perfection by St. Teresa of Ávila

5

Get Involved

There are innumerable opportunities open to the laity for the exercise of their apostolate of evangelization and sanctification.

—*Apostolicam Actuositatem*, no. 6

The Second Vatican II made clear that preaching the gospel and glorifying Christ in the way we live are not the job of the priests and other offices. In the document *Apostolicam Actuositatem* (the Decree on the Apostolate of the Laity), the Council outlines the objectives, the various fields, the forms, the external relationships, and the formulation of the lay apostolate. The document helps us recognize that the Church does not *have* a mission but *is* a mission.

> The Church was founded for the purpose of spreading the kingdom of Christ throughout the earth for the glory of God the Father, to enable all men to share in His saving redemption, and that through them the whole world might enter into a relationship with Christ. All activity of the Mystical Body directed to the attainment of this goal is called the apostolate, which the Church carries on in various ways through all her members. For the

Christian vocation by its very nature is also a vocation to the apostolate. No part of the structure of a living body is merely passive but has a share in the functions as well as life of the body: so, too, in the body of Christ, which is the Church. (no. 2)

Simply put, the laity, by virtue of their baptism, have the mission and authority by their union with Christ as the Head, to spread the gospel throughout the world (no. 3). We who are the laity, therefore, are called to attend to others.

Vatican II's *Lumen Gentium* also speaks on the laity's role:

The laity are gathered together in the People of God and make up the Body of Christ under one head. Whoever they are they are called upon, as living members, to expend all their energy for the growth of the Church and its continuous sanctification, since this very energy is a gift of the Creator and a blessing of the Redeemer.

The lay apostolate, however, is a participation in the salvific mission of the Church itself. Through their baptism and confirmation all are commissioned to that apostolate by the Lord Himself. Moreover, by the sacraments, especially holy Eucharist, that charity toward God and man which is the soul of the apostolate is communicated and nourished. Now the laity are called in a special way to make the Church present and operative in those places and circumstances where only through them can it become the salt of the earth. Thus every layman, in virtue of the very gifts bestowed upon him, is at the same time a witness and a living instrument of the mission of the Church itself "according to the measure of Christ's bestowal" (Eph. 4:7). (no. 33)

Get Involved

We who are the laity have a special purpose, indeed a vital purpose in the preaching of the gospel and in the promoting of God's kingdom "on earth as it is in heaven" (Matt. 6.10). We have a unique ability to speak to and reach the people of the world. We have a mission to bring Christ to the world and the world to Christ. *Lumen Gentium* expresses this perfectly:

> The faithful, therefore, must learn the deepest meaning and the value of all creation, as well as its role and harmonious praise of God. They must assist each other to live holier lives even in their daily occupations. In this way the world may be permeated by the spirit of Christ and it may more effectively fulfill its purpose in justice, charity and peace. The laity have a principal role in the overall fulfillment of this duty. (no. 36)

Therefore, we must see anew what the Church really is—not a building or something to attend but a real functioning body. We go to church, yes, but we *are* the Church, members of Jesus Himself. Jesus has a ministry, and that ministry works through us, the laity, with the visible structure of the Church.

In this chapter we will look at how Catholics can become more involved, particularly in small groups for study and fellowship, in third orders, and in strong marriages.

Small Groups

"For where two or three are gathered in my name, there am I in the midst of them" (Matt. 18:20). If you're not already part of a small church group, join one. If there isn't one in your parish, start one. The things we learn are meant to be talked about.

Mass is a great place for communal growth as a parish, and private prayer and worship are necessary for an individual's spiritual growth. The small group bridges these two. Its members can receive support from the group, pray for personal intentions in a circle of friends who trust each other, and grow in their spiritual lives. The nourishment that comes from small groups enriches the Christian life as the mentorship and community support help the group members grow in spiritual confidence and strength.

A small group consists of three to twelve people who meet regularly with some purpose in personal and communal growth. I suggest no more than twelve because in a larger group, people end up being overlooked or not being included, and the group misses out on the gems who are introverts.

Every group has three necessary ingredients: leadership, purpose, and meeting frequency.

Leadership is the key to the formation and success of a small group. That leadership begins with the laity, as the wonderful *Apostolicam Actuositatem* says:

> Led by the light of the Gospel and the mind of the Church and motivated by Christian charity, they must act directly and in a definite way in the temporal sphere. As citizens they must cooperate with other citizens with their own particular skill and on their own responsibility. (no. 7)

If you feel your parish needs a group that prays for its newly married couples, or if you and your friends are interested in a group that discusses the latest homily or the coming Sunday's readings, consider starting such a group. If you intend to be the group's leader, make sure you are capable and dedicated. The leader will be responsible for handling the brunt of the workload in organization, scheduling, and planning and should make sure that the group stays within the confines of its given purpose and guide it to spiritual fruition. If someone else will be the leader, make sure there is general agreement among the members on the choice of the leader. Sometimes a group member naturally assumes leadership, but if he isn't known to all the members or implicitly recognized as the leader, the group will tend to suffer.

Purpose should be kept to something of service to others and to the spiritual growth of the individual members and the group as a whole. A group of men who get together to ride jet-skis but don't meet to share some personal testimony or read some Scripture does not really promote spiritual growth. Ensure that there is a spiritual and gospel-oriented purpose to the group. One group might go from neighborhood to neighborhood mowing lawns, painting houses, cleaning up devastated areas, or otherwise serving the community with their labor. Another group might meet regularly to have breakfast together and discuss their marriage lives as sacraments and support each other with prayers and encouragement. A book-discussion club or a Bible study can be the focus of a small group. If that is something you are interested in, I recommend using a study guide that is faithful to the Magisterium and has relevant topics of discussion. Otherwise have at it!

A small group should meet as frequently as necessary. Meeting too often might not be necessary and might take people away from their family obligations, and meeting seldom reduces the nourishment that comes from meeting in a group in the first place and makes it easy for members to forget the discussion or material from the previous meeting.

Your small group should find a place to meet that fits its mood and purpose. Groups often meet at the home of one of the members, but there is always the coffee shop, where talking and engagement is encouraged, or the library or the bookstore, which offer a literary atmosphere. A place I encourage all groups to consider meeting is the parish. Your parish was inspired, planned, constructed, and is maintained as a place of fellowship and learning. And you can set aside fifteen minutes after your group's discussion to pray, listen, and just sit in the presence of the Lord in the tabernacle or in an adoration chapel.

If your parish doesn't have any small groups, consider starting one. Assemble a few like-minded folks, settle on a purpose, appoint a leader, figure out where and how often to meet, and let the Lord do the rest of the work.

Third Orders

An increasingly important opportunity for the laity to work in the Church is through third orders. These allow the laity to participate in a variety of the approved orders within the Church, such as the Franciscans, the Dominicans, and the Norbertines.

There are two divisions of third orders: the regulars, who live in convents or monasteries and take vows, and the seculars, who live in the world and make solemn promises. It is indeed a special call for the laity to be part of such distinguished groups with their rich history. Although there are many to choose from, here is a short list of the available third orders. More information can be found at the orders' websites.

• *Third Order of St. Dominic.* The Dominicans have had the benefit of lay servants since their early days. This order, founded by St. Dominic and heavily influenced by St. Catherine of Sienna and St. Thomas Aquinas, is known for scholarship and preaching. The order is very popular among scholars and those who enjoy theology and philosophy, especially teaching these disciplines. Dominicans are among the most active and organized order as well. There is a good chance that there is a Dominican chapter near you. For more information, visit: www.3op.org; www.laydominicans.com; www.laydominicancentral.org; or www.domlife.org.

• *Third Order of St. Francis and the Province of the Sacred Heart of Jesus* (www.nafra-sfo.org). Members of this order follow the example of St. Francis and work to help each other live lives in light of the Lord by committing themselves in prayer, in living in community, and in service to the poor and the neglected of the world. They offer opportunities in many parts of the United States but mainly in New York, Pennsylvania, Nebraska, and Iowa.

• *Third Order of the Servites* (www.servite.org). The Order of Servants of Mary (Servites) was founded in 1233 by seven Florentine nobles and businessmen who went to Monte Senario, outside Florence, Italy, to live lives of prayer, community, and service dedicated to Mary, Mother of Sorrows. The order is now worldwide and composed of many autonomous congregations of priests, brothers, sisters (active and contemplative), third order members, and associate members. Each congregation follows its own constitution, or rule of life, but all share the same Servite spirituality.[9] The order offers many opportunities here in the United States.

• *Third Order of the Carmelites* (www.ocarm.org). Third order Carmelites are unique in that, in addition to making the third order promises, they can and often do make personal vows of chastity and obedience according to the current state of life of the consecrated. This very enthusiastic order is made up of laity who seek to live their own vocation through lectio divina.

For those who sense a calling to one of these ways of life, third orders provide a wonderful way to gain spiritual direction,

---

[9] See http://www.ocarm.org/who-we-are/history.

discipline, and personal development and to take our faith to the world.

Marriage as a Vocation and a Sacrament

You can be more involved in the Church through your marriage. Too many times, we married Catholics look to our priests and think, "They are involved in something so holy and important, and what am I doing?" That's understandable because our culture puts so little emphasis on marriage in the areas that matter, and such great emphasis on areas that don't matter.

Listen to the words of St. Paul:

> For the husband is the head of the wife as Christ is the head of the church, his body, and is himself its Savior. (Eph. 5:23)

Because this is one of the few places in the Bible where the word *church* appears in relation to Christ, it sticks out. Together with the word *as*, which indicates "in the same manner as," Paul is using not merely a simile but a graphic image of the reality of marriage — as Christ and His Church are one, so spouses aren't separate bodies but are "one flesh," an image captured in Genesis 2:24, Mark 10:8, Matthew 19:5, 1 Corinthians 6:16, and Ephesians 5:31. This oneness and the new life that proceeds from it reflect the Trinity. Further, when others observe holy couples who pray regularly, take part in the various apostolates of the Church, show selfless love, and, most of all, respect the dignity of their vows and covenant and are faithful to them, they are attracted and inspired by such examples of strong marriages.

Not only is a strong marriage, with Jesus at the center, an example for others, but it encourages service within the marriage.

Get Involved

A couples' objectives become interpersonal, not selfish; spouses will cook or mow the lawn for different motives than just because the work needs to be done. The intention of working and making sacrifices not for *yourself* but for *your spouse* invigorates a marriage. Even sex is more enjoyable when both spouses are pleasure givers and not only pleasure receivers.

The *Catechism* calls the family the domestic church:

> The Christian *family* is the first place of education in prayer. Based on the sacrament of marriage, the family is the "domestic church" where God's children learn to pray "as the Church" and to persevere in prayer. For young children in particular, daily family prayer is the first witness of the Church's living memory as awakened patiently by the Holy Spirit. (no. 2685)

If you're a parent, certainly educating your children in the Faith is a wonderful and significant way to evangelize. And don't forget to invite your priests to your domestic church for a home-cooked meal.

The Permanent Diaconate

Deacons are not members of the laity, because they receive the sacrament of Holy Orders,[10] but they are not part of the

---

[10]Like priests, deacons lie prostrate before their bishop during ordination. There is a very humble deacon at my parish who wore the same belt for decades, and when it finally broke and he could no longer wear it, his wife celebrated. Before his ordination, his family urged him to buy new shoes because his shoes had holes in them, and they didn't want his socks to show when he lay prostrate. He refused and ended up getting three new pairs of shoes as gifts. A "holey" man, eh?

ministerial priesthood. We find deacons introduced in chapter 6 of the Acts of the Apostles, when the Twelve called together disciples who were to help preach the Word of God among other acts of service. The apostles did this because they were overwhelmed by the demands on their time.

> Now in these days when the disciples were increasing in number, the Hellenists murmured against the Hebrews because their widows were neglected in the daily distribution. And the twelve summoned the body of the disciples and said, "It is not right that we should give up preaching the word of God to serve tables. Therefore, brethren, pick out from among you seven men of good repute, full of the Spirit and of wisdom, whom we may appoint to this duty. But we will devote ourselves to prayer and to the ministry of the word."
>
> And what they said pleased the whole multitude, and they chose Stephen, a man full of faith and of the Holy Spirit, and Philip, and Prochorus, and Nicanor, and Timon, and Parmenas, and Nicolaus, a proselyte of Antioch. These they set before the apostles, and they prayed and laid their hands upon them.
>
> And the word of God increased; and the number of the disciples multiplied greatly in Jerusalem, and a great many of the priests were obedient to the faith. (Acts 6:1–7)

St. Stephen, the Church's first martyr, is the same Stephen mentioned here.

There are two types of deacons: transitional and permanent. A man who is in his last year of seminary is ordained a transitional deacon as the last step before being ordained a priest. A permanent deacon is one who can go no further in Holy Orders;

he cannot become a priest. A married man may become a permanent deacon, but he acknowledges and willingly accepts that if his wife dies, he may not remarry. Along with their vocation, many permanent deacons have a secular job, and their family (if they have one) and their job are their priority, although they are expected to commit a significant amount of time to their ministry.

Deacons have many uses, as they did in the early Church and as described in Acts 6. They are under the authority of their bishop but most often work in close association with a parish. Some serve at hospitals, others care for the sick and the elderly or minister to prison inmates; they go where they are needed. In the parish, they serve by preaching at Mass, baptizing, witnessing marriages, and leading wake services. They perform other nonliturgical activities such as heading RCIA and group studies and managing libraries. Their duties and uses are numerous and sometimes unique but most of all, they are essential. The early Church certainly thought so, and the original seven (the Magnificent Seven?) in Acts 6 have now become over eighteen thousand in the United States alone.[11] If you think you have a calling to become a deacon, speak to your pastor about this worthy way to serve the Church.

You Can Do It

Often we doubt our ability to serve, to proclaim the gospel, and to be servants of Christ. We think, "I'm not equipped to do

[11]Mark Pattison, "Number of Permanent Deacons Grows, but Many Reaching Retirement Age," Catholic News Service, August 7, 2013, http://www.catholicnews.com/data/stories/cns/1303405.htm.

that!" *Apostolicam Actuositatem* tells us how we can start: "The laity fulfill this mission of the Church in the world especially by conforming their lives to their faith so that they become the light of the world" (no. 13). Remember that God equips those whom He sends. Just as a general will not send an untrained soldier into battle, if God is calling you to do something, you can rest assured that He will provide you with the means and the ability to finish the mission.

6

Be Active in Your Parish

The only proper ecclesiology is the local parish.

— Yves Congar

Yves Congar was right. After the family unity, the parish is where the souls of the Church are formed and nurtured. The laity are intimately tied to the parish as the basic level of the apostolate and life in the Church.

The Council Fathers of Vatican II treated the subject with great care by communicating the role of the parish in the apostolate of the laity. The Council document *Apostolicam Actuositatem* reads:

> The parish offers an obvious example of the apostolate on the community level inasmuch as it brings together the many human differences within its boundaries and merges them into the universality of the Church. The laity should accustom themselves to working in the parish in union with their priests, bringing to the Church community their own and the world's problems as well as questions concerning human salvation, all of which they should examine and resolve by deliberating in common. As far

as possible the laity ought to provide helpful collaboration for every apostolic and missionary undertaking sponsored by their local parish. They should develop an ever-increasing appreciation of their own diocese, of which the parish is a kind of cell, ever ready at their pastor's invitation to participate in diocesan projects. (no. 10)

We see, then, that the laity have an invaluable part of the success of the parish. It is certainly not the sole job of the priests and deacons to operate the parish, to found new groups and begin useful initiatives. The parish, like the Church, is made up of the people who attend *and* the people who are paid to be there. Nobody is excluded. As such, members are also the people who need to participate. Attendance must equal participation, and there is much to be involved in.

In *Lumen Gentium*, the Church speaks about the laity with spirited language:

Their pastors know how much the laity contribute to the welfare of the entire Church. They also know that they were not ordained by Christ to take upon themselves alone the entire salvific mission of the Church toward the world. (no. 30)

In fact, the Council Fathers of Vatican II said in *Apostolicam Actuositatem* that the laity "have their work cut out for them":

As sharers in the role of Christ as priest, prophet, and king, the laity have their work cut out for them in the life and activity of the Church. Their activity is so necessary within the Church communities that without it the apostolate of the pastors is often unable to achieve its full effectiveness. (no. 10)

Be Active in Your Parish

The parish, your pastor, needs your help in order for the Church to fulfill her missionary duty. And you are part of that mission! Your baptism, confirmation, and life in Christ have given you the charge to carry out this mission.

The parish can start with a super website and social media suite, proper use and promotion of small groups, host apostolates, welcome bags, homily outlines, worship services, the discovery and use of parish talent with surveys, and parish book series. In this chapter I am going to discuss the fine details in imitating and executing each of these vital activities in the parish and how the laity specifically can help see them through.

A Good Website and Social Media

The Church encourages us to use media. Years before the Internet was invented, the Second Vatican Council prophetically prepared the Decree on the Use of Media in Social Communication, titled *Inter Mirifica*:

> The Church recognizes that these media, if properly utilized, can be of great service to mankind, since they greatly contribute to man's entertainment and instruction as well as to the spread and support of the Kingdom of God. (no. 2)

However, Vatican II did not have clergy exclusively in mind when they promulgated this document. Addressing pastoral activity in the use of media, *Inter Mirifica* states:

> All the children of the Church should join, without delay and with the greatest effort in a common work to make effective use of the media of social communication. (no. 13)

Notice that the Church urges all of the faithful to empower their missionary voice with the use of social media. With this apostolate specifically, parishioners can play an active and dynamic role in the success of their parish.

Since this document was written, Pope Paul VI started a mission that continues to this day; it is known in the Church as World Media Day. Each year there is a new publication addressing the use of media and its effect on evangelization. These short documents contain powerful insight and direction and have been added to by Popes Paul VI, John Paul II, Benedict XVI, and Francis.

The use of the Internet and social media is vital for evangelization. The song "Go Tell It on the Mountain" reminds us that on a mountain we can speak in all directions, for many ears to hear. The Internet and social media are like a mountain in this digital age. Brandon Vogt, content director for Word of Fire, put it perfectly when he said, "Fulton Sheen or St. Augustine would have given their right arms for the power that we have with these digital tools."[12]

It is likely that close to 100 percent of your parish has access to the Internet. Therefore it would behoove your parish to invest in an informative and professional-looking parish website, if it doesn't already have one. It would be fair to consider the website to be one of the most important outreach apostolates or ministries that your parish can offer. A good parish website has more than contact information, Mass times, the reconciliation schedule, and a PDF of the bulletin. It should be the hub for all information on promoting participation and catechesis.

Here are just a few things that your parish website should have:

[12] Brandon Vogt, *Life on the Rock*, February 13, 2014, https://www.youtube.com/watch?v=JLIr3p4LiPw.

- A blog: find someone in your parish (maybe you and a group of people) who can make a small contribution every now and then to keep your parishioners engaged.

- An access library: the website needn't contain loads of content; it can link to other trusted sites where that content can be found—for example, the *Catechism*, Church documents, recommended books, videos, and so forth.

- Information for groups, events, and sports leagues.

- A page to welcome and announce new members, the newly baptized, and the newly married.

- A donation page, where a monthly contribution can be made: believe it or not, this is almost an unspoken demand. People find it much easier to give online, one time or recurring, rather than writing a check and licking an envelope or remembering to bring cash to Mass.

- Frequently asked questions—not just about the parish, but also about apologetics.

This is a short list; it is by no means where your parish could or should stop with its website content.

Remember that the parish website is a 24-7 extension of the parish office. It might also be the first place someone will go before visiting the parish whether he is new in town or not. Therefore, it is crucial that the website be attractive and well maintained. Colorful graphics, easy navigation, and content are the three musts for a good website. I have included in the resource section some Catholic site designers who specialize in parish websites.

Next, your parish should make use of social media, such as Facebook, Twitter, and Google+. These are not replacements for your website, but are easy, free, and useful. These tools offer constant engagement with your parishioners, your audience, and especially the youth.

Your parish can start with a Facebook page and post content that will speak well to its parishioners. Twitter is a site that will allow your parish to make announcements with a maximum of 140 characters. This conciseness allows readers to skim through the content in a breeze. Google+ is a good tool for creating social circles. It also allows users to stream live video using Google Hangouts On Air. (See the resources for a link to a Google Hangouts On Air how-to.)

The key to social media is good content. People will "like" your parish's Facebook page, "follow" your parish on Twitter, and "join" your parish on Google+ because they'll know it is a parish of the Catholic Church. Therefore, it should post things Catholic:

- Links for catechesis and apologetics

- Links to the blogs and websites of parishioners

- Announcements of events

- Daily readings

- Links about the saint of the day, special Mass schedules for holy days, and so forth

- Pictures of sacred art from around your diocese

- Lectures by guest speakers

- Live video stream of the Mass

- Fundraising competitions or opportunities

- Baptisms, funerals, and other family events for those who cannot make it

Be Active in Your Parish

Social media is the future of evangelization and catechesis. It is popular and easy to use and offers a good opportunity for parishioners themselves to promote their parish. If you're adept at using social media, speak with your pastor about setting up something for your parish and maintaining it, perhaps in collaboration with fellow parishioners. Or maybe you could find others to take on this task.

Whatever you do, don't quit. It takes time to implement a social media plan. Be creative, ask parishioners to "find you" with their account, and stick with it.

If you don't think you can find someone to handle all this, consider that Internet and social media are multibillion-dollar industries, and although the Internet has been around for a while, there is a rapidly growing demand for web designers, code writers, bloggers, and social media managers. Your parish could advertise for pro bono help from someone who could add the experience to his résumé.

Inter Mirifica summons us:

> To provide for the needs [of social media], priests, religious, and laymen who are equipped with the proper skills for adapting these media to the objectives of the apostolate should be appointed promptly. (no. 15)

Perhaps you have those skills and could handle your parish website or social media pages. I can tell you from personal experience that such volunteer work is the key to getting experience, getting to know the right people, and building a platform of your own. All it takes is a few hours a week, and you might find that you are really good at it and really enjoy it as well. In time, you could see yourself switching careers or starting your own apostolate. It is highly unlikely that when you present this information and idea to your parish staff, they will turn you down. So go out there and get it done!

Small Groups, Again

In the previous chapter, I wrote about small groups, but I also want to talk about how small groups can be encouraged by the parish. There are many ways that the parish can promote such groups, but the bottom line is that they must be promoted in the first place. The pastor and his team must take a leadership role in ensuring that parishioners are encouraged to participate.

During one Lent, my pastor decided to have a series of homilies, given by different priests and deacons, on various forms of prayer. The series was a hit, and the parishioners enjoyed hearing a consistent message every week on something specific they could do to be better Catholics. Not just saying, "Go do it," those priests and deacons had a small table and a chair, sat down, and actually showed the parishioners *how* to pray. They became the example!

Imagine, though, a series of homilies on spiritual growth through small groups: over the course of a few weeks, the whole parish could be educated quickly and become eager to join a small group with a purpose. The effect would be just like that of the homilies on prayer: parishioners would go home educated on the topic and confident in what they were doing and would also have a clear purpose and direction to move forward. This is one of the ways your parish can promote small groups. In their leadership role, the pastor and his team can speak about how to host a small group and participate in one. Your parish can also host short seminars on how to start and host a small group. If that isn't practical, an instructional video can be produced and uploaded to the parish website.

Be Active in Your Parish

A group that discusses the Mass readings or homilies is a good way to start. The parish can offer handouts or post PDF documents with notes on the readings or the homilies, and small groups can meet weekly and follow along with the same notes as everybody in the parish. This is a perfect way for the parish to grow together.

Once some small groups have been established, the parish can promote them by making an announcement about the groups and inviting parishioners to sign up for one (or more) after Mass. In the narthex or in the back of the church or somewhere that is easy for people to get to once Mass has ended, have labeled tables set up where parishioners can sign up. Members of each group can man the tables and answer questions about the groups.

Parish-based small groups have an advantage over private ones because they bring together people who don't know each other but have common interests, and this can be more effective for growth and for encouraging people to get to know more than the same five to ten people in the parish. Priests and deacons can further support small groups by attending their meetings occasionally for fellowship and to lend encouragement. From experience I can tell you that this is a sure way to keep parishioners happy. It's not just about making an appearance; it's important for parishioners to know that their priests and deacons acknowledge and are involved and interested in what they are doing. And actions can speak louder than a homily.

Small groups work: they build community, create leaders, give people a sense of belonging, and promote spiritual and personal growth. If you're interested in taking action on this, talk to your pastor and fellow parishioners about getting a small group started.

Host Apostolates

In the introduction, I mentioned a pastor who said that greeting parishioners takes precedence over the collection. *That's* host-ing—hospitality. Hosting can take form in many ways, including a team of greeters. Some parishes have teams of greeters who arrive well before Mass on their scheduled days to greet all who come through the door with a warm, inviting smile and say, "Good morning! Welcome to St. Such and Such!" Greeters should be present after Mass, to hold the door, see parishioners off, and let them know that the parish looks forward to seeing them the next week. It's great when priests stop to greet parishioners after Mass, but it's important to involve the laity in this ministry too.

Host apostolates do not have to stop there. The laity in the parish should ask themselves, "In communion with our pastor, how are we helping people feel at home?" New parishioners and visiting Catholics want to see this sort of thing. They want to be acknowledged, they want interaction, and they want to find a place to return to each week. More importantly, they need to be inspired by the lay members of the parish to do something in the Church and be happy doing it as well. This is contagious, and the benefit for any parish will be noticeably brought to fruition with happy faces and retained members.

The first few times I attended Mass, nobody gave me a single look or gesture or greeting until the sign of peace. It wasn't until I had attended Mass a few times that my friend Sean, who had helped me convert to the Catholic Church, sat with me and explained things to me and introduced me to the pastor and the associate pastor after Mass. This was invaluable to my conversion and my sense of belonging. That extra step that Sean took—going out of his way to attend a different Mass from the one he usually attended with his family—went a long way toward giving me confidence that there was somebody at Mass who actually wanted me there.

Weeks later, after I had been there a few times but hadn't been confirmed yet, I saw an individual who looked as if he didn't know what was going on and was not Catholic. It took some guts, but I gathered up my courage and asked him if he was a member of our parish, to which he responded no. I offered him a bit of encouragement because I was a convert on the way as well. He went on to attend RCIA and is now an active member of our parish.

A small act of hospitality, encouragement, and acknowledgment goes a long way. When we acknowledge people, we immediately give them a sense of belonging and value. That said, hospitality is not just up to the priest or the deacons or the ushers or even those volunteers who greet people at the door. It's up to every Catholic in the pew and in the narthex to greet others and make them feel welcome, even if only by smiling or holding the door.

New Parishioner Welcome Bag

An idea that goes a long way in outreach to new parishioners and new converts is a welcome bag, which gives new members some items to familiarize them with the parish, help them in their faith journey, or even reignite their faith altogether. It could be a plastic bag or tote with a Bible, a prayer book, some study material, the latest bulletin, a welcome letter from the pastor, a rosary, and a survey (see page 88 for details on the survey). There is no limit. The welcome bag brings the Church into the home of newcomers. By setting new members up with the tools they need, the parish equips them to jump into their faith feet first, with confidence, and with gratitude (for all the free stuff, if nothing else!).

Outline of the Homily for Notes

Call me naive or call me ignorant, I don't mind, but the first time I walked into a Catholic Church while seeking my conversion, I looked around for a paper with the outline of the service and picked up the paper from a pile before entering through the narthex. Of course, I didn't understand the structure of the Mass. To add to my confusion, when I got to my pew, I looked at the paper I had picked up and saw that it was a coloring page! It was to keep kids busy! It made me laugh at myself, but I didn't know how to follow the Mass and became frustrated. A couple of weeks later, when my friend Sean let me sit with him, he grabbed a book, flipped to a page with that day's date, and gave the book to me.

He said, "This is the missal."

"Missile? Okay, so these people are terrorists who use books to cause damage," I thought.

I soon understood the blessing of the missal. I found it incredible that every Catholic in the world is quite literally on the same page. But where was I supposed to write my notes? The homily was great, but I didn't have a journal to keep and certainly didn't anticipate the contents of the homily. What was I to do?

This isn't to sound smug or sarcastic, but I don't think most of the people in my parish have a stereophonic memory, if that's even a thing. Parishioners can't remember *everything* the priest or deacon says during the homily. We need something to take notes on. Yes, each person can bring his own journal, but it would be efficacious in every sense to have a handout that gives a basic outline of that Sunday's readings and lines for taking notes on the homily. We also know the power of supply. If you supply it, more people will use it. If more people were taking notes, more people would have something to take home and remind them throughout the week of what they learned on Sunday.

Add to that the power of note-taking and memorization, and you've got a recipe for real spiritual growth. If you want to memorize something, you write it down. That significantly increases your memory every time — just as when you make a good slap shot or throw a great spiral, you remember how to do it, how it feels, and can articulate how to do it if someone asks. It works the same with spiritual food. So my suggestion to the parish is this: print an outline of the readings and make sure there are several lines for note-taking. People will use this, and it will increase your parishioners' spiritual growth by oodles (an actual measurement, I promise).

Nonliturgical Worship Services

One of the most beneficial services a parish can offer are song and praise sessions. With a band that plays contemporary music, a solo vocalist, or even a CD of recorded music, these sessions offer the opportunity to stand, sit, jump, raise hands, hold hands, whatever — all to connect with God and praise Him.

Another way to worship God outside of the Mass is the supreme experience of eucharistic adoration. Some parishes have small chapels dedicated to perpetual adoration; if your parish has one, I strongly suggest making use of it. In our busy and ever-demanding world, what could be better than a few moments' rest, not thinking about any of your lively demands, concentrating only on the God of the universe brilliantly exposed right in front of you? I know it might be tough to grab an hour from your schedule, but it doesn't have to be an hour. Go for a short time and work your way from there. What's important is going at all, praying, and being silent for a moment or two.

Some parishes combine musical worship with eucharistic adoration: musicians play familiar hymns or contemporary songs with the Eucharist exposed. This adds another dimension to worship.

Survey of Talent

"They should not cease to develop earnestly the qualities and talents bestowed on them in accord with these conditions of life, and they should make use of the gifts which they have received from the Holy Spirit."[13] Your parish might be home to 2,500 Catholics or 25 Catholics. No matter the number, a significant number of families and individuals want to do something. They might not know what it is they want to do, but they are itching to help out or just need to be nudged in a direction. Many are pleased to be asked by their pastor or associate pastor to head some ministry.

The problem is that the pastoral team doesn't always know exactly what talents exist in the parish or who is interested in which ministries. When this happens, there are missed opportunities. A great solution to this problem is to use a survey of talent.

This simple form can be given out over the course of a month or so to poll the parish for interest in the different existing ministries: children's choir, choir director, brass instrument players, gardeners, door-to-door evangelizers, eucharistic ministers, greeters, and so forth. A special comment section can be added so parishioners can add their own ideas and interests that aren't listed.

[13] *Apostolicam Actuositatem*, no. 4.

Be Active in Your Parish

This became an interesting topic for me once. When I was on a team that visited parishioners on behalf of the pastor, one gentleman, nice as could be, told me that all he wanted to do was be a lector at Mass once a month. He went to daily Mass and weekly adoration, but what was missing in his life was a way to give back. It was a small task to take that request back to the pastor. A survey of talent gathers similar data for the pastor and eliminates the problem of not knowing where various parishioners could serve best.

The survey can be implemented immediately. Coordinate this with your parish's pastoral team and assemble a document that describes the needs of the parish. Find some parishioners who are willing to gather the results and present them to the pastoral team. From there it will be easy to reach out to the parish members who expressed interest in certain ministries. Find a leader for the group—someone with good organizational skills, leadership experience, and enthusiasm—and have him take the reins of the group with guidance and oversight from the pastoral team.

Creative Nonfiction Book Series

Everyone likes a good conversion story. I mentioned testimonies in an earlier chapter, and this is where a testimony can be used in the parish: to make a book.

There are a number of small publishers that your parish can hire to gather and author the testimonies of members of your parish in the style of creative nonfiction. Creative nonfiction might be an unfamiliar term, but you've likely read it before. It is a style in which an author communicates a true story accurately but shapes it to read like a fictional story. In short, it's the true story of real people, written really well.

I have belonged to churches that use this for both fundraising and evangelization. In fact, my story of recovery from an addiction is in a book called *Sufficient to Stand*. It started with a simple survey in which our pastor asked parishioners who were willing to tell about their addictions to indicate it in fifty words or less. Selections were made, and those individuals spent some time on the phone with their assigned author and told their story. The author, in so many words and days, wrote the story accurately, and in a matter of weeks, our parish made the book available for purchase. The church sold hundreds of copies at five dollars a book and gave those with addictions hope and solace for their own journey.

This is a powerful tool that your parish can utilize immediately. With a good plan, an initial investment would give your parish a way to connect with its parishioners, have people share their stories, change lives, and raise money. If it were up to me, in addition to a *Catechism* compendium, I would give this sort of book to RCIA candidates and catechumens, because long after the dogma and the rites have been learned, people will either remember or forget the love of Jesus they have experienced in the months it takes to enter the Church. This is the way to make a lasting impression on your new and existing members.

Possible topics are countless. I've seen books on specific conversions, such as from atheism; reversions to the Church; addictions; and various Catholic life experiences in general. With a book like this, your parish will grow in holiness, interest, knowledge, and fellowship. These testimony books make people feel welcome and unjudged, knowing that someone else in their parish has walked the same road they have. As people buy this book and give it to others, love, hope, and faith are shared and spread.

Be Active in Your Parish

A number of publishers can do this for your parish (see the resources for one example). If you've got the talent within your parish (remember that survey?), your parish doesn't even need a publisher; the parish could just hire or ask for a volunteer to be the creative author to tell these stories and then self-publish the book.

Conclusion

Work for Unity among Christians

*All, though in different ways, long for
the one visible Church of God, a Church
truly universal and set forth into the world
that the world may be converted to the Gospel
and so be saved, to the glory of God.*

—*Unitatis Redintegratio*, no. 1

This book has laid out specific and detailed means for us to become better evangelists and more active and involved Catholics. We've learned the essentials of building a personal testimony to tell others about Christ in our lives and how much He loves us. We've discussed the need to have a real and lasting relationship with Jesus and what exactly that entails for a Catholic. We've considered many things that we as individuals can do to take part in the harvest of souls and the betterment of the Church as well as things that can revive a parish as a place where souls are served and souls can serve. I want to conclude with an echo of the Church's communication on proper and sound ecumenical dialogue.

The Church has discussed the issue of unity in every age. Jesus spoke to His Father about our oneness; Fathers of the Church such as Cyprian made points on efforts to maintain unity (*Unitate Ecclesiae*, no. 6), and since the Reformation we have had encyclical letters from Popes Clement XIII, Pius IX, Leo XIII, and John Paul II. We can see that this is an ongoing concern of the Church and that it reflects our Lord's own request to the Father:

> I do not pray for these only, but also for those who believe in me through their word, that they may all be one; even as thou, Father, art in me, and I in thee, that they also may be in us, so that the world may believe that thou hast sent me. The glory which thou hast given me I have given to them, that they may be one even as we are one, I in them and thou in me, that they may become perfectly one, so that the world may know that thou hast sent me and hast loved them even as thou hast loved me. (John 17:20–24)

Pope Clement XIII made ecumenism the subject of his first encyclical letter, written in 1758. He referred to the crisis of unity as a "bitter and constant concern" (*A Quo Die*, 1), going on to tell how those who are sons of light differ from those who are sons of the world for their willingness to maintain the bonds of unity (*A Quo Die*, 3).

In the mid-nineteenth century, Pope Pius IX wrote the encyclical letter *Inter Multiplices* to the archbishops and bishops of France, pleading for unity. In this letter, much as in this book, the wise pope did not just state the mere need for unity, but offered specific guidance as to how such a unity is achieved and maintained. Most recently, as I've cited many times in this book, the Second Vatican Council and Pope John Paul II took to this matter at length with splendid words of wisdom.

In short, the principal aim of ecumenism is to create unity among God's people. Ecumenism is banding together, joining forces, and creating an environment conducive to cooperation among Christians, although it is not a compromise of faith.

Christians are already unified in our belief in the saving grace and work of Jesus Christ's Passion, death, and Resurrection. We have that, and we need to maintain it and at the same time move forward in dialogue and activity concerning doctrine and liturgy.

The issues at stake cannot be tossed aside as unimportant. The Second Vatican Council recognized this, reminding us that the divisions of Christians, each claiming to be the true followers of Christ, are contradicting the will of Christ (*Unitatis Redintegratio*, no. 1). Some would refer to our differences as "spine issues," where the central idea of God is shared, but the specific matters are less important. Surely, Jesus delivered a different message. To our Lord and King Jesus, the issues of baptism and Holy Communion, among others, are not spine issues. These are His words on the subject, not mine:

> Truly, truly, I say to you, unless you eat the flesh of the Son of man and drink his blood, *you have no life in you.* (John 6:53; emphasis mine)

> Truly, truly, I say to you, unless one is born of water and the Spirit, *he cannot enter the kingdom of God.* (John 3:5; emphasis mine)

Gratefully, the Church recognizes the validity of baptism, subject to the correct formula (Matt. 28:19), even if the individual does not believe in the proper effects of a valid baptism (*Catechism of the Catholic Church*, no. 1278).

The same is not true of Holy Communion. Protestants who choose not to believe that the consecrated bread and wine are the actual Body and Blood of Jesus might convince themselves, as with baptism, that even if they are wrong, they are only misled and are still partaking in the reality. Even if that were the case, which it is not, it is nullified because the Protestant is not receiving a consecrated host. They can have all the ignorance, but the reality of these sacraments remains with or without their belief.

One can see how dogma matters and that the ecumenical dialogue between Catholics and our separated brethren must include copious conversation on our faith. Such dialogue, when carried on with charity, will build on the foundation we already have. To echo Vatican II's Decree on Ecumenism, *Unitatis Redintegratio*, Catholic Faith must be discussed frequently and explained more fully and more often in such a way that Protestants can understand (no. 11). Therefore, because it is the matters of doctrine that have created an impasse, we are obligated to move forward with our family in discussion of religious matters, and to do so with preciseness and charity.

We are called to be the salt of the earth and the light of the world (see Matt. 5:13–16). That force gives illumination to society and flavor to culture. Therefore, we have an obligation not to keep our religion to ourselves but to share it with the world for its own good.

This effort toward unity with brotherly love is what Jesus said is the entire message of the law and the prophets and concerns the greatest command all:

> When the Pharisees heard that he had silenced the Sadducees, they gathered together, and one of them [a scholar of the law] tested him by asking, "Teacher, which commandment in the law is the greatest?" He said to him, "You shall love the Lord, your God, with all your heart, with all your soul, and with all your mind. This is the

greatest and the first commandment. The second is like
it: You shall love your neighbor as yourself. The whole law
and the prophets depend on these two commandments."
(Matt. 22:34–40)

In this divine command, we learn just how to *fill our Father's
house*: love God first, and let that love lead us to love one another
as we love ourselves.

My heart is bent toward the conversion and unity of the
whole Church. I dream of the day when Catholics and Protestants reach a final and perpetual unity in our Lord, who binds us
and gathers us to Himself. Before His Passion, He had one thing
on His mind and lips and heart: "Holy Father, keep them in thy
name, which thou hast given me, that they may be one, even as
we are one" (John 17:11).

"There is no doubt that the Holy Spirit is active in this en-
deavor and that he is leading the Church to the full realization
of the Father's plan, in conformity with the will of Christ."[14]

For more reading on ecumenical dialogue with our Protestant
brothers and sisters, I recommend the following:

Unitatis Redintegratio (Decree on Ecumenism), Vatican II

Ut Unum Sint ("To Be One") by Pope John Paul II

Euntis in Mundum ("Go into the World") by Pope John
Paul II

*Rebuilt: Awakening the Faithful, Reaching the Lost, and
Making Church Matter*, by Fr. Michael White and Tom
Corcoran

---

[14]Pope John Paul II, *Ut Unum Sint*, no. 100.

Filling Our Father's House

Documents from the Pontifical Council for Promoting Christian Unity (http://www.vatican.va/roman_curia/pontifical_councils/chrstuni/index.htm)

Useful Tools and Resources

My website (www.shaunmcafee.com)
On my personal website I blog, podcast, post resources, and more. In this book I cite Vatican II documents extensively. I recommend to all a full, prayerful reading of these documents, but for those who do not have time, head over to my site for concise summaries of the pertinent details in the documents.

USCCB Daily Readings (http://www.usccb.org/bible/readings/)
Here you'll find the daily Mass readings in word and audio as well as great reflections. The website will automatically bring you to the present day's readings, and there is also a calendar to find readings for a different day. http://www.usccb.org/bible/readings/

Blue Letter Bible (www.blueletterbible.com)
This Scripture discovery website hyperlinks each word and verse of the Bible to translations, definitions, commentaries, etymologies, and more. This is a great tool that's free.

St. Paul Center for Biblical Theology (www.salvationhistory. com)
Scott Hahn's nonprofit research and educational institute promotes life-transforming Scripture study in the Catholic tradition.

Holy Apostles College and Seminary's Massive Open Online Course (MOOC; www.hacsmooc.cc)

Discover free four-week courses on theology, bioethics, social teaching, and much more.

Third Order Websites

Dominicans: www.3op.org, www.laydominicans.com, www.laydominicancentral.org, or www.domlife.org.

Franciscans: www.thefriars.com and www.franciscanstor.org for Regular and find Secular information at www.nafra-sfo.org

Servites: www.servite.org

Carmelites: www.ocarm.org

Catholic Website Design

eCatholic (www.ecatholicwebsites.com) is a one-stop shop for beautiful, modern, easy-to-manage parish websites.

Catholic Web Company (www.thecatholicwebcompany.com) can help you form a unique and functional parish website.

Google+ On Air Hangouts and more.

Learn how to stream videos online easily through Google+; this may be used for RCIA, funerals, baptisms, and more: http://www.google.com/+/learnmore/hangouts/onair.html.

Publishers for Parish Books

Good Catch Publishing (www.testimonybooks.com) is a creative nonfiction publisher that can write and print your parish book in order to evangelize and raise money.

Amazon Self Publish (https://kdp.amazon.com) lets you edit and submit your own book for Kindle.

Useful Tools and Resources

Bezalel Books (www.bezalelbooks.com) is a Catholic publisher that will edit, print, and publish your title.

Lulu (www.lulu.com) is a rather unique service that offers self-publishing, drop-shipping services, and a storefront for writers and publishers. Lulu makes it possible for any parish, group, or individual to produce, print, sell, and ship beautiful books with ease.

About the Author

Shaun McAfee is a convert to the Catholic Faith. He works for the U.S. Army as a civilian and is the Director of Marketing and Content for Holy Apostles College and Seminary and the Social Media Administrator for Patrick Madrid's Envoy Institute. He is a proud graduate of the University of North Dakota with a B.S. in Aeronautics and earned a Master's in Business Administration at Liberty University. He is working toward a Master's in Dogmatic Theology at Holy Apostles College and Seminary and expects to graduate in May 2015 and is in the process of becoming a Lay Dominican. He loves blogging, podcasting, and creating resources to help others understand, live, and defend the Faith at his website, www.shaunmcafee.com. He is happily married with two beautiful children and lives in Omaha, Nebraska.

An Invitation

Reader, the book that you hold in your hands was published by Sophia Institute Press. Sophia Institute seeks to nurture the spiritual, moral, and cultural life of souls and to spread the Gospel of Christ in conformity with the authentic teachings of the Roman Catholic Church.

Our press fulfills this mission by offering translations, reprints, and new publications that afford readers a rich source of the enduring wisdom of mankind.

We also operate two popular online Catholic resources: CrisisMagazine.com and CatholicExchange.com.

Crisis Magazine provides insightful cultural analysis that arms readers with the arguments necessary for navigating the ideological and theological minefields of the day. *Catholic Exchange* provides world news from a Catholic perspective as well as daily devotionals and articles that will help you to grow in holiness and live a life consistent with the teachings of the Church.

Sophia Institute Press also serves as the publisher for the Thomas More College of Liberal Arts and Holy Spirit College. Both colleges provide university-level education under the guiding light of Catholic teaching. If you know a young person seeking a college that takes seriously the adventure of learning and the quest for truth, please bring these institutions to his attention.

www.SophiaInstitute.com
www.CatholicExchange.com
www.CrisisMagazine.com